T. H. Green's Moral and Political Philosophy

T. H. Green's Moral and Political Philosophy

A Phenomenological Perspective

Maria Dimova-Cookson

First published 2001 by
PALGRAVE
Houndmills, Basingstoke, Hampshire RG21 6XS and
175 Fifth Avenue, New York, N. Y. 10010
Companies and representatives throughout the world

PALGRAVE is the new global academic imprint of
St. Martin's Press LLC Scholarly and Reference Division and
Palgrave Publishers Ltd (formerly Macmillan Press Ltd).

ISBN 978-0-333-91445-8

This book is printed on paper suitable for recycling and made from fully managed and sustained forest sources.

A catalogue record for this book is available from the British Library.

Library of Congress Cataloging-in-Publication Data
Dimova-Cookson, Maria, 1967–
    T.H. Green's moral and political philosophy : a
    phenomenological perspective / Maria Dimova-Cookson.
        p. cm.
    Includes bibliographical references and index.
    ISBN 978-0-333-91445-8
    1. Green, Thomas Hill, 1836–1882—Contributions in political science. 2. Ethics, Modern. 3. Phenomenology.
    I. Title.

JC223.G8 T5 2001
128'.4'092—dc21

00–069475

10   9   8   7   6   5   4   3   2   1
10   09 08 07 06 05 04 03 02 01

To Susan and Brian

Contents

List of Abbreviations   x

Preface   xi

Introduction   1

1. Green's view of the method of moral philosophy   5
2. Husserl's critique of the sciences   9
3. Linking the phenomenological reduction to a theory of
   human practice   15
4. Applying the phenomenological reduction to moral
   philosophy   20

1 Green's Transcendental Theory of Human Practice   23

1.1 Defining the term 'transcendental'   24
1.2 Green's metaphysics of knowledge   27
1.3 Hume's discovery of the 'world of spirit'   32
1.4 The spiritual principle that underpins human
    practice, or Green's theory of the will   40
1.5 Why Green's principle is in fact a transcendental rule   45
1.6 Applications of Green's transcendental rule   48
1.7 The difference between transcendentalism and spiritual
    determinism   51

2 Green's Phenomenological Moral Theory   55

2.1 Similarities between Green and the utilitarians   57
2.2 The difference between the pursuit of pleasure
    and the pursuit of the moral good   61
2.3 The moral ideal as the perfection of man   64
2.4 The phenomenological circle   67
2.5 The change of perspective   70
2.6 Between deontology and consequentialism   72
2.7 Is it the individual or her perfection that is an end in
    itself?   74

| | 2.8 Moral vulnerability and negative morality | 76 |
| | 2.9 Conclusion | 78 |

3 Green's Theory of the Common Good — 81

	3.1 Outlining the two perspectives in defining the common good	83
	3.2 The common good as personal moral growth	85
	3.3 The salvation argument: criticisms and defence	87
	3.4 The unique position of the self	92
	3.5 The loss of the concept of the ordinary good	97
	3.6 The common good in the second sense: as a society of equals	100
	3.7 Conclusion	102

4 Positive and Negative Freedom: Green's Contribution to the Debate — 105

	4.1 Juristic freedom and moral freedom	108
	4.2 Positive freedom and negative freedom	115
	4.3 Which freedom is more important?	124
	4.4 Conclusion	127

5 Rights in Green's Political Theory: Universal or Historical? — 129

	5.1 The concept of social recognition	132
	5.2 Practical social recognition	133
	5.3 Metaphysical social recognition	137
	5.4 Green's theories of human agency and morality: need as a sufficient justification of rights	140
	5.5 Rights as an expression of negative freedom: negative and positive morality	143
	5.6 Rights – universal or historical?	145
	5.7 Conclusion: reconciling the two lines of thought in Green's philosophy	146

Conclusion	**149**
Notes	151
Bibliography	167
Index	173

List of Abbreviations

Prolegomena	T. H. Green, *Prolegomena to Ethics*
Principles	T. H. Green, *Lectures on the Principles of Political Obligation*
Freedom	T. H. Green, 'On the Different Senses of "Freedom" as Applied to Will and to the Moral Progress of Man'
Liberal Legislation	T. H. Green, 'Lecture on "Liberal Legislation and Freedom of Contract"'
The Crisis	Husserl, *The Crisis of European Sciences and Transcendental Phenomenology*
Meditations	Husserl, *Cartesian Meditations*
Treatise	Hume, *A Treatise of Human Nature*

Preface

There was a time when I believed idealism was the most interesting aspect of philosophy. I have not lost this belief, but now I have started to see that the ideas that I find attractive can also be subsumed under different titles, including transcendentalism, pragmatism, practical philosophy, existentialism and, indeed, realism. Exponents of these types of philosophy will insist that their theories are not idealist, for the term 'idealism' is quite unpopular. I think this reveals a lack of awareness about the historical origins of ideas that are otherwise widely accepted. T. H. Green (1836–82) saw himself as an idealist partly because he belonged to the Kantian and Hegelian traditions. He explained human practice in terms of the pursuit of particular ideas. Therefore, if we are to analyse human practice, we must understand the nature of the ideas that individuals pursue in their actions. Green's principal concern was to counterbalance the naturalistic and the utilitarian theories that interpreted human behaviour in terms of simpler or more complex responses to pain and pleasure. The phenomenological interpretation of Green offered in this book aims to reveal the significance of his theory in the field of moral philosophy. It also casts Green's contribution to political philosophy – a contribution that is more widely recognised – in a new light. The phenomenological approach uncovers Green's subtlety in defining the nature of human agency, moral motivation and the shift in definition of the moral good, depending on whether we refer to its agent or its recipient.

I discovered T. H. Green while preparing my MA in political philosophy at the University of York. I was lucky to be able to take Peter Nicholson's course on the political theory of the British idealists, as this course was not offered every year. The interest in phenomenology I brought with me from Sofia University, where Zdravko Popov ran a reading group and we discussed Husserl's *Crisis of European Sciences* section by section. My book is based on my DPhil thesis (submitted to the University of York in 1998), which explores the connections between phenomenology and the philosophy of T. H. Green. There has been an additional year and a half of research, revising and improving the original thesis by taking into account many comments and suggestions from specialists in British idealism and in political theory more generally before this book was completed. The two people who have helped me most, and who have been there for me throughout this time, are Peter Nicholson, my DPhil supervisor, and Richard Cookson, my husband. Peter is a brilliant scholar as well as a caring and attentive supervisor. He has gone through the greatest number of drafts, always giving me prompt and constructive feedback. My discussions with him and my reading of his own work have improved my understanding of Green and have taught me how to think and how to structure my work. Richard's help with my work has been academic as well as personal. He has read many drafts of the chapters, encouraging me to express my thoughts more clearly, and indeed, in better English. He has been my role model and my best friend. It is impossible to express how indebted I am to him.

Most of the revisions of the original thesis are based on the detailed and penetrating comments of my external examiner, Andrew Vincent. He has given me advice and has commented on more recent revisions of the different chapters. I also owe special thanks for the feedback I have received from David Boucher, James Connelly, John Horton, Duncan Ivison, Susan Mendus, Krassimir Stojanov, Giuseppe Tassone, Colin Tyler and Lilian Alweiss. I have benefited considerably from the long and fruitful discussions at the political theory seminar at York Politics Department by the questions and comments of Tom Baldwin, Frank Brogan, Alex Callinicos, Matt Carter, Jonathan Davies, David Edwards, Gordon Finlayson, Steven Holland, Matt Matravers, John Maynor, Monica Mookherjee, Stamatoula Panagakou and Christian Piller. I have been fortunate to meet and discuss aspects of my work with Alan Milne, Avital Simhony, Timothy Sprigge and William Sweet. I would like to thank Susan Cookson and Sabine Kim as well as Ruth Willats for their subtle and magical editorial touch. I was able to continue my work on this project thanks to my Postdoctoral Fellowship awarded by the British Academy.

Finally I would like to express my gratitude to my international family. I have dedicated this book to my parents-in-law who have provided me with the most loving environment away from my home country. They have also proof-read my work time and time again. I would also like to say thank you to my parents, and to pay tribute to the memory of my uncle, who died tragically days before I completed this book. The three of them are people who, in their own way, have increased the welfare of my native town, Burgas.

Introduction

As a British idealist, T. H. Green (1836–82) belongs to the traditions of both Anglo-American and European philosophy. From the British empiricists and utilitarians he has taken their accessible logic, engagement with politics and aspects of utilitarian theory. As for the German idealists, Green shares their concern with the work of human consciousness and the belief that human spirit defines the nature of human practice. To a large extent Green's originality lies in combining the achievements of German philosophical thought with the practicality and clarity characteristic of British empiricism and utilitarianism. With this synthesising approach Green advances philosophical idealism to a higher stage. I shall argue that he develops a theory of human practice and a theory of morality which can be defined as phenomenological. We can thus see Green not only as a British Hegelian, but also as a British phenomenologist referring to the phenomenology founded by Edmund Husserl (1859–1938). While the association with Hegel places Green's philosophy in the eighteenth century, the association with Husserl positions him in the first half of the twentieth century. The significance of Husserlian phenomenology will be addressed in sections 2, 3 and 4 of this introduction. It is the purpose of the whole book to demonstrate the advantages of interpreting Green's philosophy in a phenomeno-logical context.

Green and Husserl shared the view that the method of natural science was inappropriate to philosophical research. They were not only advocating two separate methodologies for the natural sciences on the one hand, and for the human sciences, on the other; they also believed that the method of natural science was based on a philosophical misconception of the world. Their defence of a radically different approach to philosophy can be linked to the 'Copernican turn' made by Kant, who claimed that understanding structures nature.[1] Knowledge is a human construct; therefore, our vision of what nature is is influenced by the way human consciousness works. Advocating a new method for philosophy (in the case of Green, for moral philosophy) was underpinned by the belief that the spiritual has priority over the physical world. This view, that we have to employ two completely different methodologies in researching the social world on the one hand, and the physical world on the other, was also expounded by Wilhelm Dilthey (1833–1911), Wilhelm Windelband (1848–1915), Heinrich Rickert (1863–1936) and later by Alfred Schutz (1899–1959). What is specific to Green and Husserl, however, is that they both analysed the dynamic of personal spirituality. While phenomenologists such as Schutz were more interested in social action and the different types of social relationship, the power of Green and Husserl resides, to a large extent, in their insights into the processes that take place within the individual's consciousness. Husserl, in particular, has been criticised for failing to present a convincing account of intersubjectivity and, more generally, for underestimating the role of the external world in human practice. A full defence of Husserl's phenomenology can be a project in its own right. However, as Green's philosophy addresses social and political issues in depth, such a criticism cannot apply to him, and therefore it is not imperative to deal with it here. What is important is that both Green's and Husserl's philosophy offer a development of and improvement on Kantian transcendentalism, in the sense that they see the transcendental function of subjectivity not in terms of fixed categories, but in terms of a dynamic process of personal transformation. More about this will be said in sections 2, 3 and 4 which briefly present and offer an interpretation of Husserl's phenomenology.

This book addresses Green's theories of human practice, morality, the common good, freedom and rights. It aims to revise and extend our understanding of a great philosopher who has a recognised position in the history of political thought, but who, for number of reasons, has been sidelined from the mainstream accounts of the history of philosophy. Here I have undertaken the ambitious task of interpreting Green's philosophy along phenomenological lines, and thus of exploring ideas that were implied but not developed by Green himself. I criticise some aspects of his philosophy and draw attention to others, pointing out where his originality is to be found. By taking a strong stance on Green's philosophy, I risk incurring the disapproval not only of those who object to Green's work, but also of those who support it. I have two justifications for my pro-active approach. First, my purpose is to revive philosophical interest in Green and I believe that by developing further some of his main theories, I am serving this purpose. Secondly, it has been Green's own philosophy that has inspired me to take further the questions he dealt with and some of those he left unanswered.

Having said that Green's philosophy is largely marginalised, I should also point out that there has been a recent revival of interest in his work. When Melvin Richter wrote his book on Green in the 1960s, British idealism was among the least popular subjects.[2] However, in the 1980s and 1990s scholars including Rex Martin, Alan Milne, John Morrow, Peter Nicholson, Raymond Plant, Avital Simhony, Geoffrey Thomas, Colin Tyler, Andrew Vincent, David Weinstein and others were writing about Green and establishing an academic environment of interest in the British idealist's philosophy. What is also encouraging is that Green's philosophy has been seriously addressed by the analytical philosophers David Brink and Thomas Hurka.[3]

This book examines Green's understanding of human agency and the nature of moral behaviour, and the last two chapters apply this understanding to an analysis of his views on freedom and rights. In Chapter 1, I argue that Green's theory of general human practice is a transcendental theory. His claim that in all her desires an agent is an object to herself[4] is, on analysis, a formal rule of human practice. Green's theory explains the dynamic interaction between 'will', 'thought' and 'desire' and their formative role with respect to human practice – a theory much more acceptable than Green's 'metaphysics of knowledge' in which only 'thought' is seen as a pre-conditioning factor of human behaviour. Chapter 2 addresses Green's moral theory preceding the introduction of the theme of the common good. I argue that Green effectively introduces two definitions of morality: a formal and a substantive one. He argues that we behave morally if we act with 'good will', that is, if we pursue an object of our will in a self-disinterested manner. However, he also argues that the moral nature of our conduct depends on the character of the object we pursue: we act morally only if we pursue the 'unconditional good'. To explain the complex relation between good will and the unconditional good – complex, because Green used both in turn as an absolute criterion of moral action – I introduce the concept of the 'phenomenological circle'. The upshot is that the change of perspective from which one defines morality results in two different definitions. The importance of registering the employment of two different perspectives – and the criticism of Green for failing to account for the change – is central to this book. In Chapter 3 where the 'common good' is analysed, we see again that Green ends with two, not one, concepts of the common good as a result of shifting between two perspectives. While the first concept reflects a process of personal moral growth, the second reflects a substantive vision of the common good: a society of equals. In the first sense the common good represents moral good, while in the second, substantive sense, it represents ordinary good. I criticise Green for neglecting the concept of ordinary good, and therefore for not giving an account of the dialectic between moral and ordinary good.

This dialectic is what underpins the relation between positive and negative freedom – a discussion which is the focus of Chapter 4. There I analyse Green's theory of freedom against the background of the debate on positive and negative freedom. Green's philosophy has much to offer this debate. Green develops a theory about the different senses of freedom by speaking about 'juristic' and 'true' freedom. I argue that the two (positive and negative) usages of freedom in the realm of the political are underpinned by the two different senses of freedom in the realm of personal experience (the 'juristic' and 'true' freedoms). The dialectic between moral and ordinary action elucidates the interdependence between juristic and true freedom; it suggests a new, formal account of the difference between positive and negative freedom; and it provides the philosophical tools with which we can evaluate which of the two freedoms is more important under which circumstances.

Chapter 5 discusses Green's theory of rights. This chapter brings together and compares the conclusions reached in Green's moral philosophy with those reached in his political theory. I argue that these theories offer two justifications of human rights – one on the basis of need, the other on the basis of social recognition. Green himself does not reconcile these two grounds for justifying rights, but with a little additional reconstruction his philosophy can offer a resolution. What might be seen as an inconsistency within his overall philosophy represents, in essence, a genuine dilemma: is the individual obliged to contribute to social welfare or, alternatively, is he the ultimate goal of social progress? I argue that Green's philosophy carries the potential to resolve this dilemma by leading to the observation that human morality has both a negative and a positive dimension.

In the remaining part of this introduction I will deal with issues that I will not address directly in the book. As the book focuses mainly on Green, it does not explore Husserl's phenomenology or the parallels between Green and Husserl. Therefore, I will use the introduction to provide the preliminary information necessary for the project of analysing Green's philosophy in a phenomenological light. I will discuss Husserl's phenomenology and the features common to the two philosophers. The next two sections address, in turn, Green's and Husserl's critiques of the natural sciences. In the case of both men this critique is strongly connected to the theories they expounded. Both Green and Husserl aspire to the same ideal of philosophical knowledge: rational and rigorous on the one hand, but having the theoretical equipment to understand and explain the nature of human spirit on the other. Husserl's *Critique of the European Sciences* represents his final attempt to elucidate his phenomenological theory; it therefore gives not only a negative, but also a positive idea of what phenomenology is.[5] Section 3 offers a brief exposition and interpretation of the 'phenomenological reduction' and clarifies the way in which phenomenology should be understood for the purposes of this book. Finally, in section 4, I analyse the moral character of the phenomenological reduction, that is, I apply the phenomenological theory to moral philosophy – something that Husserl did not do, but Green did.

1.   Green's view of the method of moral philosophy

The *Prolegomena to Ethics* (hereafter *Prolegomena*) is Green's major philosophical work.[6] It is based on his lectures delivered between

1878 and 1882. Green died before he completed his work on the book and the manuscript was passed to A. C. Bradley, who divided the *Prolegomena* into books, chapters and sections and composed their titles. Book I and part of Book II were published in *Mind* 7 (1882).[7] In the Introduction Green discussed his intention to write a treatise on moral philosophy and the difficulties that he would face in fulfilling this task.

Green believed that there should be a proper philosophy of morality and spirit. Neither natural science nor dogmatic theology could serve this purpose. Each was failing to cover one of two necessary requirements: first, an understanding of the uniqueness of the human spirit; and second, a belief in the importance of rational knowledge. Natural scientists believed in rational knowledge, but not in the life of the spirit. Poets and theologians believed in the life of the spirit, but they were not aiming at rational, systematic and clear knowledge. Green, who believed in both, found himself in a unique position. At the time when he started his work on the *Prolegomena* moral questions had been either marginalised or, if tackled by science, dealt with inappropriately. In the Introduction to this major philosophical work Green spoke in more detail about the two opposed tendencies he had to counterbalance.

The first tendency was represented by 'the multitude of the educated',[8] who viewed moral issues, elevated feelings and matters of spiritual sophistication with utter seriousness, yet believed that they were properly the province of poetry and theology. This tendency expressed a new academic fashion, according to which moral philosophy belonged to the past ('Moral Philosophy is a name of somewhat equivocal repute; ... it commands less respect among us than was probably the case a century ago').[9] It testified to the increased popularity of science among those who considered themselves intellectuals. However, this popularity was accompanied by a scepticism with respect to the possibility of a serious rational enquiry concerning moral issues. People such as Green who attempted to rationalise morality were out of step with the spirit of the time and their efforts were 'likely to seem something of an anachronism'.[10] Educated men who saw themselves on the cutting edge of intellectual progress did not think they were underestimating the issues related to higher spirituality. They believed that natural matters and morals were two discrete sides of life: the first could be treated scientifically, while the second should be dealt with only by poets:

> The most intelligent critics had rather, it would seem, that the ideas which poetry applies to life, together with those which form the basis of practical religion, should be left to take their chance alongside of seemingly incompatible scientific beliefs, than that anything calling itself philosophy should seek to systematise them and to ascertain the regions to which they on the one side, and the truths of science on the other, are respectively applicable. 'Poetry we feel, science we understand'; – such will be the reflection, spoken or unspoken, of most cultivated men ...[11]

Green found this attitude disturbing, and saw a problem behind the seemingly successful division of labour between the sciences and poetry. He was 'alarmed at this dangerous juxtaposition' which seemed so natural to his progressive contemporaries: 'Such men seem little disturbed by the admission of a joint lodgement in their minds of inferences from popularised science, which do not admit of being reconciled with these deeper convictions in any logical system of beliefs.'[12] The problem was that nineteenth-century science did not sit easily with an elevated approach to the human spirit. One could not accept the two simultaneously with any degree of consistency. For men of science – 'the most cultivated men' – the exclusion of moral issues from science was, in practice, a way of marginalising them.

So we can see that Green's project to lay a foundation for a philosophy of ethics would not be met with enthusiasm by intellectuals with a penchant for poetry and who regarded man as a spiritual being. But Green had to confront something worse. There were scholars who did not see any obstacle to why science should not deal with moral issues, but to whom poetry and religion were of no substance when human nature was discussed, or even of no substance altogether. The second tendency which Green wanted to counteract was represented by those who believed that 'a physical science of Ethics' was not impossible.[13] Among these he included anthropologists, evolutionists, representatives of 'a scientific "Cultur-geschichte"'[14] and utilitarians. The tendency to explain moral behaviour by recourse to a set of external circumstances and basic psychic faculties was gaining more and more popularity. To all intents and purposes, human personality was reduced to matters of fact, and such matters of fact would easily be subjected to scientific observation and experiment.

A scientific approach to morality was a relatively recent phenomenon. However, Green felt that this undesirable turn in moral enquiry was not solely the fault of contemporary scientific fashions. 'Simplifying' spiritual nature had precursors in the moral philosophy of the past. Here Green's reference is to the English empiricists:

> The questions raised for us by the Moral Philosophy which in England we have inherited, are just such as to invite a physical treatment. If it is the chief business of the moralist to distinguish the nature and origin of the pleasures and pains which are supposed to be the sole objects of human desire and aversion, to trace the effect upon conduct of the impulses so constituted of action, and to ascertain the several degrees in which different courses of action, determined by anticipation of pleasure and pain, are actually productive of the desired result; then the sooner the methods of scientific experiment and observation are substituted for vague guessing and an arbitrary interpretation by each man of his own consciousness, the better it will be.[15]

The best British moral philosophy had come up with were the concepts of moral sense and of free will. If those had been tackled properly, the possibility of natural science having a voice in the field of morality would have been prevented. Unfortunately for Green, they were not. Green believed moral philosophers' failure – and Hume's in particular – to assess the role of reason in the process of moral motivation, had resulted in a general image of human nature that could be subjected further to scientific treatment.

One particular problem with the scientific approach was its tendency to retrace moral attitudes to their 'roots'. In practice this meant a regressive enquiry into the animal aspects of human nature. This trend was given a massive push by 'the evolutionists',[16] who extended the enquiry from the limits of one life span to those of many human generations. With unhidden sarcasm, Green tells us how the evolutionist doctrine of hereditary transmission can explain 'how susceptibilities of pleasure and pain, of desire and aversion, of hope and fear, may be handed down with gradually accumulated modifications which in time attain the full measure of the difference between the moral man and the greater ape'.[17] Green did not object to historical research into culture. What he was suggesting was that there should be limits to how far back in human development we have to go. If we undertake such research with the purpose of analysing morality, going back to 'the antecedents of the moralised man'[18] would be pointless. The problem with evolutionism is its tendency to reduce 'the moral susceptibilities of man to the rank of ordinary physical facts';[19] the problem with natural science in general is 'the scientific impulse to naturalise the moral man'.[20]

As was the case with intellectuals who thought moral philosophy out of fashion, Green found an internal inconsistency in the position adopted by the natural science moral philosophers. They acknowledged the necessity of moral norms; they recognised the fact that a phenomenon such as 'moral behaviour' exists; and they believed that people *should* strive towards it. Green, however, saw a conflict between their attempt to explain human spirit in naturalist terms and their ambition to assert the necessity of moral norms. These two – the naturalised account of human nature and the belief in ethical laws – Green found irreconcilable: 'to a being who is simply a result of natural forces an injunction to conform to their laws is unmeaning.'[21] A system of moral laws can be meaningful only against the background of a 'moral account' of human nature. Such an account Green offers in Books II, III and IV of his *Prolegomena*.

To sum up: Green was not content with the two prevailing approaches to dealing with moral issues. Neither using the methods of natural sciences, nor leaving ethical life in the hands of poets and theologians was acceptable to him. Green disapproved of the division of labour between science and religion where the first applied to nature and the second to human affairs. In an age where the role and importance of sciences were developing very quickly, this division led to neglecting the significance of ethics. We find a very similar conclusion in Husserl's critique of the sciences.

2. Husserl's critique of the sciences

While Green's dissatisfaction with natural sciences forms part of his introduction to the *Prolegomena*, Husserl's critique of sciences was one of the main themes of a book that comprised his final attempt to explain the meaning of phenomenology.[22] In *The Crisis of European Sciences and Transcendental Phenomenology* (hereafter *The Crisis*) Husserl argues that because of the growing popularity of natural sciences, 'objectivity' has become synonymous with 'truth', while 'subjectivity' has been associated with 'relativity', 'lack of precision' and 'uncertainty'. As a result, everything related to human subjectivity has been seen as lacking scientific value, or even, serious significance. People have become oblivious to the fact that science has its foundation in 'pre-scientific' life, that its purpose and meaning are derived from the context of private individuals' lives. Therefore, Husserl argues, the foundations of human knowledge should not be sought in technical formulas and scientific laws, but in the structures of subjective experience. I will present Husserl's critique of sciences in more detail for two reasons: to allow the reader to find those elements that are similar to Green's own critique, and to disclose some of the main thrusts of Husserl's phenomenology.

Husserl claims that the European sciences are in crisis with the full awareness that this is a paradoxical claim: 'how could we speak straightforwardly and quite seriously of a crisis of the sciences in general – that is, also of positive sciences, including pure mathematics and the exact natural sciences, which we can never cease to admire as models of rigorous and highly successful scientific discipline?'[23] Yet, there is a crisis signalled by the fact that the sciences have lost their importance in people's lives; Husserl refers to 'the "crisis" of science as the loss of its meaning for life.'[24] In the Vienna lecture he declares that '[t]he European nations are sick' and the sciences are unable to offer a cure.[25]

Husserl argues that the belief that the pure sciences are not meant to deal with existential problems is misguided. It is the result of nineteenth-century positivistic attitudes that sciences have ceased to be 'dependent branches of the One philosophy'[26] and have become 'mere factual' sciences. Once positivism has reduced the function of science, then a huge range of 'questions of the meaning or meaninglessness of the whole of human existence'[27] are left outside the purview of science:

> The exclusiveness with which the total world-view of modern man, in the second half of the nineteenth century, let itself be

determined by the positive sciences and be blinded by the 'prosperity' they produced, meant an indifferent turning-away from the questions which are decisive for genuine humanity.[28]

We can see that Husserl's concern is similar to Green's. The fact that human affairs have been left outside the purview of science has produced negative consequences: intellectuals have turned away 'from the questions which are decisive for genuine humanity'. Husserl argues, however, that the positivists' interpretation of the task of science is only a recent phenomenon. It was not always the case that science was detached from 'all questions vaguely termed "ultimate and highest"'.[29] At the dawn of its full glory – at the time when Galileo instigated mathematised physical science – science had an ambitious task. As a branch of philosophy, it shared philosophy's ideal of rational systematic knowledge capable of guiding people's lives by providing answers to all important questions. The ethos of Europe was shaped by this ideal of knowledge. The collapse of this ideal brings Europe to a state of crisis – which Husserl identifies as a 'European' problem.[30]

Galileo was the founding father of mathematised natural science. Husserl reminds us that when the new science was emerging in Galileo's day, its purpose was not seen in its narrow positivist interpretation. Science was not meant to cover certain aspects of human life only, while ignoring others. Science was seen as creating the paradigm of what is rational in general. After leading us through these considerations Husserl summarises his idea of the crisis concisely and clearly in the following lines:

This is a crisis which does not encroach upon the theoretical and practical successes of the special sciences; *yet it shakes to the foundations the whole meaning of their truth.* ... For the primal establishment of the new philosophy is ... the primal establishment of the modern European humanity itself – humanity which seeks to renew itself radically, as against the foregoing medieval and ancient age, precisely and only through its new philosophy. *Thus the crisis of philosophy implies the crisis of all modern sciences as members of the philosophical universe*: at first a latent, then a more and more prominent crisis of European humanity itself in respect to the total meaningfulness of its cultural life, its total '*Existenz*.'[31]

The idea that the crisis of philosophy also implies a crisis of the modern sciences is not new to Husserl, but it is only in *The Crisis* that he presents it so forcefully. In his Vienna lecture, delivered only six months before the lectures on which *The Crisis* is based, he maintains the idea that, unlike the sciences which are immensely successful, it is only philosophy and the humanistic disciplines that are in crisis.[32] He held the crisis of philosophy, not the crisis of science, accountable for the crisis of European culture.

Husserl's purpose in reviewing Galileo's scientific output is twofold. First, he wants to reveal Galileo's importance to the forma-tion of the European spirit. 'What is new, unprecedented, is the conceiving of this idea of a rational infinite totality of being with a rational science systematically mastering it.'[33] Secondly, he wants to find out where exactly things have gone wrong; to trace how this task has been fulfilled by Galileo himself and those who came later. Galileo started out on the right track, but he was the first to lose his way. He discovered the correlation between natural events and mathematical formulas and thus introduced the mathematisation of physical nature. This formalisation of physical science proceeds with the arithmetisation of geometry. Thus scientific research could proceed entirely as a work with formulas and numbers. This is where things have gone wrong, according to Husserl. By entering the ground of symbols, formulas and numbers, knowledge becomes 'a sort of *technique*'. It starts to operate according to fixed rules and is no longer driven by its original motives. The rules of symbolic logic are independent of the 'rules' of intuitive scientific thinking, because 'the *original* thinking that genuinely gives meaning to this technical process and truth to the correct results is excluded'.[34]

One can work in the sphere of technical thought no matter whether one carries the original scientific ethos of seeking knowl-edge that provides rational guidance in human life in all of its aspects. The problem here, according to Husserl, is not in the method of 'technisation' (*Technisierung*), but in the fact that this method can be performed in ignorance of the original scientific task. The original intention for research is now detached from its performance. This is what Husserl means when he claims that the arithmetisation of geometry 'leads almost automatically, in a certain way, to the emptying of its meaning'.[35] Once again, Husserl states the problem with sciences in a general and concise way, making the same point as mentioned above, yet taking it a step further:

> Actually the process whereby material mathematics is put into formal-logical form, where expanded formal logic is made self-sufficient as pure analysis or theory of manifolds, is perfectly *legitimate*, indeed necessary; the same is true of the technization which from time to time completely loses itself in merely technical thinking. But all this can and must be a method which is understood and practised in a fully conscious way. It can be this however, only if care is taken to avoid dangerous shifts of meaning by keeping always immediately in mind the original bestowal of meaning [*Sinngeung*] upon the method, through which it has the sense of achieving knowledge about the world.[36]

When Husserl speaks of 'shifts of meaning' he refers to the process by which the original intention of a scientist is forgotten and superseded by another. The original meaning of science is not in its technical method, but in the purposes of the everyday, pre-scientific life. Therefore science has achieved its aims, not by exercising the method of technisation, but by providing solutions to problems of human life in general. It may seem that Husserl's critique emphasises a trivial consideration. 'Yet this triviality has been buried precisely by exact science' as scientists do believe that physics represents *the* truth about nature.[37] This naive belief, Husserl says, has become 'a living historical fact'.[38] Husserl takes up a familiar theme – he is not the first to develop a critique of science. However, he presses his charges persistently by extending his analysis into the cultural implications of the problem.

A 'substitution of idealized nature for prescientifically intuited nature' has taken place as a result of Galileo's mathematisation of natural science.[39] Mathematised science has changed people's perception of nature and of the world in general: the world has become a series of formalised entities. In a certain sense science has alienated the world from us; it has dehumanised it. This has occurred because scientific method does not require awareness of the origins of its meaning or of its consequences. 'What was lacking, and what is still lacking, is the actual self-evidence through which he who knows and accomplishes can give himself an account, not only of what he does that is new and what he works with, but also of the implications of meaning which are closed off through sedimentation or traditional-ization ...'[40] The nature of scientific method was such that it con-cealed an important factor: the process through which science acquired meaning from pre-scientific life. A whole domain of reality remains unobserved: the domain of the 'life-world'. 'The life-world can be disclosed as a realm of subjective phenomena which have remained "anonymous".'[41] The realm of the life-world ontologically precedes the realm of science. Science functions in such a way that it keeps the existence of the life-world permanently hidden. Galileo was at once a genius of discovery and of concealment – 'he discovers what has since been called simply the law of causality, the "a priori form" of the "true" (idealized and mathematised) world, the "law of exact lawfulness" according to which every occurrence in "nature" – idealized nature – must come under exact laws'. However, 'this is a discovery-concealment, and to the present day we accept it as the straightforward truth'.[42]

Mathematised natural science has led us to the conviction that we can only be certain of what is 'objective'. Entities with a fixed and easily formalisable character have acquired higher ontological status, while those related to human individuals and human culture are seen as less credible and less trustworthy:

> In his view of the world from the perspective of geometry, the perspective of what appears to the senses and is mathematizable, Galileo *abstracts* from the subjects as persons leading a personal life; he abstracts from all that is in any way spiritual, from all cul-tural properties which are attached to things in human praxis.[43]

This reduces nature to mere physical bodies. Thus the method of science influences the character of the very objects of scientific research: if initially (by the intention of its original task) science addressed the whole of nature, subsequently, throughout its progress, science has reduced the scale of its object to mere bodies. The scientific method has become a method of 'objectifying' the things it deals with. 'What characterizes objectivism is that it moves upon the ground of the world which is pregiven, taken for granted through experience, seeks the "objective truth" of this world, seeks what, in this world, is unconditionally valid for every rational being, what it is in itself.'[44] Objectivism is the attitude of perceiving the world as a combination of bodies; of believing that truth and certainty are qualities that belong only to entities that are not 'in any way spiritual'; of neglecting, therefore, all aspects of reality that belong to human nature. Husserl counterbalances objectivism with an attitude of inquiring into the 'subjective structure' of human experience. Husserl calls this attitude 'transcendentalism'.

Transcendentalism is the philosophy that inquires into subjective experience, into the processes through which things around us acquire their meaning. In general terms, transcendentalism is a shift from objectivity to subjectivity, from 'physicalistic naturalism'[45] to the realm of the life-world. 'Thus it is not the being of the world as unquestioned, taken for granted, which is primary in itself; and has not merely to ask what belongs to it objectively; rather, what is primary in itself is subjectivity, understood as that which naively pregives the being of the world and then rationalizes or (what is the same thing) objectifies it.'[46]

To recap: Husserl does not share with Green only the conviction that scientific method is inapplicable in the field of 'all that is in any way spiritual'. He claims that the nature of scientific method is such that it 'purposefully' ignores or bypasses 'cultural properties that are attached to things in human praxis'. Science overshadows the 'life-world' (the 'realm of subjective phenomena') from which it receives its purpose. A reversal of priorities is required. Instead of turning our gaze away from subjectivity in our pursuit of truth, we should focus our research on it.

3. Linking the phenomenological reduction to a theory of human practice

I will explain the idea of phenomenology by presenting and reinterpreting Husserl's theory of the phenomenological reduction, a procedure which he also calls *epochē*.[47] I argue that phenomenology is not to be found in the conclusions reached by the *epochē*, but in the theory of human practice implicit in Husserl's theory of the phenomenological reduction.

Husserl wants to demonstrate that scientific methodology is necessarily related to the way the human mind works. Knowledge is pursued and developed by individuals and all scientific discoveries have taken place as personal insights. That is why epistemology

should investigate the work of human consciousness and the structure of personal experience. Husserl develops the theory of the *epochē* which describes the particular mental steps one should undertake if one wants to engage in scientific thinking. The purpose of this exercise is that the scientist, or philosopher, abandons all presuppositions, in order to acquire clarity of vision. Husserl believes that the purpose of both science and philosophy is the attainment of absolutely certain knowledge. Because this is an extremely difficult task, the procedure through which we are able to achieve it is demanding. As we shall see, the performance of the *epochē* bears a resemblance to religious conversion.

The beginning of the *epochē* consists in a process of suspending our belief in the existence of the objective world. This is not easy because, Husserl admits, '[m]ore than anything else the being of the world is obvious'; the 'world incessantly stands before our eyes, as existing without question'. However, *'our experiential evidence of the world* lacks … the superiority of being the absolutely primary evidence'.[48]

Husserl believes that we acquire 'primary evidence' only when we 'set aside' everything which raises the slightest doubt about its own authentic existence. Husserl uses many terms to describe this 'setting aside'. He speaks of bracketing, suspending, becoming disinterested. The person who undergoes the *epochē* is not supposed to deny the obvious, but to question prior attitudes towards everything in the surrounding environment. When Husserl claims that we should 'doubt' or 'suspend belief' in the existence of the world, he means that we should try to detach ourselves from our standard and habitual perceptions of the objects around us. Husserl observes that believing in the existence of the world implies performing many routine activities: all our 'judgings', 'valuings', 'position takings' are based on, or imply, an unquestioned belief in the existence of the world.[49] So, in order to suspend this belief, we should abstain from getting involved in our routine actions. After the *epochē*, all things in the external world continue to reside in their places, but the person who has performed the *epochē* is personally detached from them. Suspending belief in the world implies changing the ways we are involved with it.

As a result of the suspension of our belief in the existence of the world, we acquire 'pure living, with all the pure subjective processes making this up'. To explain these pure subjective processes Husserl refs to Descartes' concept of *cogito*.[50] By this term Husserl attempts to capture all the basic activities of human consciousness: 'to think', 'to experience', 'to perceive', 'to remember', 'to see', 'to apprehend' – 'Descartes, as we know, indicated all that by the name *cogito*.'[51] The idea is similar to Descartes' '*cogito ergo sum*': once we have suspended belief in the existence of the objective world, all we have left is our capacity to see, to think, to apprehend. This is what we cannot place in doubt as this is the doubting agency itself. However, as opposed to Descartes, Husserl believes that what we are left with as ultimately beyond doubt is not simply 'myself'. 'I', as a person, also belong to the objective world, so 'I' am one of those things that has been suspended. Husserl introduces the distinction between the 'psychological' and the 'transcendental' ego. After the *epochē* I have divested myself of my psychological ego and have reached my transcendental ego. By discovering the *cogito*, or by attaining one's transcendental ego, anyone who has performed the *epochē* has gained apodictic evidence that the existence of the world is secondary to the existence of the transcendental consciousness; the world has become 'absolutely nothing else but the world existing for and accepted by [him] in such a conscious *cogito*'.[52]

My purpose here is to explain the meaning of phenomenology on the basis of Husserl's theory of the *epochē*. Phenomenology is a type of philosophical analysis which is displayed by the process of phenomenological reduction. We can see that by performing a phenomenological reduction we 'destructure' what we have already 'structured' in the course of everyday life. Let me explain. Husserl claims that the phenomenological reduction demands the suspension of belief in the existence of the world. He defines the life one has led before the *epochē* as 'natural existence'. By describing the particular actions a person has to do in order to perform a phenomenological reduction, Husserl in essence offers an analysis of human practice. All those things that the *epochē* is supposed to suspend are things which we do in the normal course of life. Husserl offers a very interesting analysis. He observes that in their spontaneous life people tend to value, judge, create stereotypes, take things for granted. People tend to 'objectify' things; that is, they tend to create things and then take their existence for granted. For example, all value judgements, opinions, 'position takings' are phenomena that have emerged from human practice and, according to Husserl, they do not have independent apodictic existence. However, because of their nature, people tend to take things for granted as they are, without accounting for the fact that these things are products, rather than entities in themselves.

The idea that human consciousness works in such a way that it constantly produces new phenomena is also to be found in Husserl's critique of European sciences. In the previous section we saw how in *The Crisis* Husserl develops the thesis that Galilean science has replaced real nature with an idealised and mathematised nature. The general certainty that physical nature exists is no longer arrived at (due to the influence of Galilean science) as a result of spontaneous interaction with nature, but as a consequence of the educated view that nature is what it is because its existence is based on natural laws.[53] European sciences have the tendency to 'objectify' things, to ascribe to them the status of certain existence. The same tendency can be found in human nature in general. The problem arises from the fact that scientists, and people in general, are unaware of that process. The purpose of the *epoché* is to 'paralyse' this spontaneous activity of producing new things so that one can see what is of absolute, authentic existence. The phenomena in the world are not authentic precisely because they are 'made'. The only authentic thing is the activity which produces them, and this is the activity performed by the transcendental consciousness. The transcendental consciousness or the transcendental ego is the only thing that is not 'preconditioned' because it preconditions everything else.

We do not have to go along with Husserl in all his assertions. But I believe that his theory offers us enough to grasp the nature of phenomenological analysis. We can see that the idea of the phenomenological reduction is based on a certain understanding of the nature of human practice. Husserl expresses the view that in their spontaneous behaviour people tend to create stereotypes, values – all kinds of new phenomena – which they subsequently start to treat as things taken for granted. People live in a world full of things which they have created and the existence of which they do not question. Husserl notes that many of the existing phenomena, rather than being absolutely valid or absolutely obvious, have a quite complex nature and heterogeneous contents. They have their origin in people's experience, and accordingly their meaning is not solid and necessarily obvious, but is 'derived'. On the basis of this observation, Husserl argues that in order to understand the meanings of things, we have to 'track down' the process by which they have been created.

Phenomenology is both a method and a theory of human nature. As a method it implies research into the process through which a phenomenon has acquired its current meaning, that is, an attempt to uncover the subjective attitude that has ascribed to this phenomenon its meaning. As a theory of human nature it stresses the fact that human practice is based on the work of human consciousness and thus has a subjective origin. Accordingly, the meanings of all the 'objective' phenomena of the human environment are to be seen only in the context of human experience, and the latter is by nature subjective. Chapter 1 demonstrates that Green explains human practice as a dynamic process of self-objectification, a theory that is very close to the understanding of human practice implied in the phenomenological reduction.

Husserl's phenomenology is a transcendental theory of the Kantian type as it aims to articulate the particular functions of the transcendental consciousness which *precondition* the whole of human experience.[54] The advantage of Husserlian philosophy over Kantian is to be found in the fact that phenomenology suggests how the gap between 'pure' consciousness and experience can be bridged.[55] Husserl's theory of the phenomenological reduction indirectly shows that a philosopher can gain a vision of the work of 'transcendental' consciousness only through an experiential act: the *epochē* is a method which has to be performed; it has to be personally enacted. In his *Meditations* Husserl claims that '[e]verything that makes a philosophical beginning possible we must first acquire by ourselves'.[56] His concern not only with the structure of transcendental consciousness, but also with the *articulation of the method* of philosophical research (the phenomenological reduction), draws our attention to the fact that knowledge is part of human practice and thus 'pure' knowledge is impossible. As we shall see in Chapter 1, Kant's distinction between *a priori* and *a posteriori* knowledge is based on the false belief that the metaphysics of knowledge is separate from, and prior to, the metaphysics of general human practice. I will argue that in a similar way to Husserl, Green contributes to the transition of transcendental philosophy from its stage of asserting dichotomies between the *pure* work of consciousness and experience, or between the transcendental and the psychological, towards a 'transcendental' philosophy which analyses the conditions of human practice in the light of the particular private and social experiences the individual has gone through.

4.   Applying the phenomenological reduction to moral philosophy[57]

The purpose of Husserl's *epochē* is to help philosophers arrive at 'primary evidence' – the only evidence that is, according to Husserl, absolutely unequivocal. His task is epistemological as he is concerned with truth and the procedure that leads to certain knowledge. However, he does not explore the application of the phenomenological reduction in moral philosophy, and this is a field where, I believe, it has significant potential. Husserl claims that the *epochē* effects 'a complete personal transformation, comparable in the beginning to a religious conversion'.[58] This observation opens a different avenue of possible applications: the *epochē* offers us insights into the nature of human practice; it can also be applied to moral theory.

The phenomenological reduction is a process of putting aside all our personal involvements with the surrounding world, all our habitual dispositions and routine assumptions. It is a process of overcoming those elements of our experience that are related to our exclusively personal circumstances. It is a procedure through which we rise above our ordinary, everyday situation of being dependent on a variety of changing factors as a result of which we adopt a meta-position. We step outside the involvements in life that make us fickle and largely unpredictable. This procedure is, in principle, the same as the process of acquiring moral motivation. In Chapter 2 we shall see that, according to Green, moral action consist in adopting a self-disinterested disposition. He speaks of morality as the process of overcoming one's desires for immediate satisfaction and developing desires for the pursuit of the common good. The phenomenological reduction registers our capacity to suspend our habitual self-centred disposition. This will be discussed at length in Chapters 2 and 3. The *epochē* gives us an insight into the phenomenology of moral action.

While Husserl wanted to establish the conditions of a 'disinterested spectator',[59] Green's moral philosophy can be described as defining the conditions of a 'disinterested agent', that is, a moral agent. By placing the phenomenological reduction in the context of an ethical theory we are in a better position to see its universal character. For Husserl the transcendental reduction is a procedure that aims to suspend those aspects of subjectivity that are relative and contingent, and thus to uncover the underlying transcendental subjectivity that is universal. Husserl's *epochē* is introduced in a purely epistemological context and philosophers have been concerned that it could lead to extreme relativism. Questions have been raised about why one philosopher should believe the insights of another's phenomenological reduction. The assumption is that everything that is subjective is always relative and never universally valid. However, if we understand the *epochē* as the personal transformation inherent in moral action, we can see its universality in at least two ways. First, it is universal because it reflects the formal conditions of moral behaviour. Secondly, the acts of a moral agent carry universal value. Before performing an *epochē* (or prior to moral conduct) an agent is an ordinary agent and his actions are relatively good in the sense that they are good to the extent that they bring him some satisfaction. However, we do not view an agent's moral conduct as relatively good. Being moral implies acting according to a universally accepted standard. The relative goodness that exists prior to the phenomenological reduction is superseded by the universal goodness that follows it.

To sum up: I have argued that Husserl's phenomenological reduction can be applied not only in the field of epistemology but also in the field of moral philosophy. We shall see that Green's moral theory exemplifies this application.

1
Green's Transcendental Theory of Human Practice[1]

In Book I of his *Prolegomena*, 'Metaphysics of Knowledge', Green comes across as a somewhat heavy-handed idealist; however, in Book II, 'The Will', he develops an original transcendental analysis of human nature. I shall refer to his theory of 'the will' as the theory of 'human practice'. Green's claim, that in all his desires an agent pursues an idea of himself, represents, on analysis, a transcendental rule of human practice. Green takes Kantian transcendentalism and develops it further. Kant had established a rigid dichotomy between pure thinking, on the one hand, and experience, on the other. Thus Kantian transcendentalism asserts the formative role of pure, *a priori* categories and denies transcendental status to all human faculties other than thinking. Green's philosophy takes the transcendental idea and develops it by offering a better explanation of the mental setting that creates the format for human practice. According to Green, human behaviour is not preconditioned by our instincts or natural forces, but by an interplay of 'will', 'thought' and 'desire' – an interplay that can be rendered in a formula.

Green believed that his theory of knowledge (in Book I) would pave the way for his main task of explaining the spiritual nature of human practice (in Book II). In other words, he started his *Prolegomena* with a 'metaphysics of knowledge' because he believed that thought was primary to human experience. In this chapter it will become clear that Green's theory of human practice demonstrates that it is not only thought that has a role in the transcendental setting of human behaviour. The sharp division between thought and experience, which Green inherited from earlier philosophers – both empiricists and idealists – and which constitutes the core of his theory of knowledge, is no longer to be found in his theory of practice. So one of my main tasks in this chapter is to demonstrate that Green's philosophical originality is to be found in the second, not in the first, and thus to show that much of this originality has not been brought to light precisely because his epistemology contains philosophical statements that contradict the more powerful insights of the theory of the will. I shall argue that his epistemology fails to fulfil its initial task as it gives either wrong, or strongly one-sided, accounts of Green's own philosophy.

However surprising it may seem, a good introduction to Green's analysis of human nature and spirituality is the philosophy of David Hume. There are two main themes in Hume that are coherent with, and therefore anticipatory of, Green's own ideas. First, Hume's critique of reason is strikingly similar to Green's critique of natural sciences. Reason, according to Hume, is simple, mechanical and impotent in both the field of knowledge and of morals. Human life is diverse and complex and it is not thinking but passions that play a central role. Green develops a similar attack not against reason, but against the methods of natural science. His thesis that natural science is ill-equipped to deal with ethics expresses a similar philosophical belief about the totality of human spirit. Secondly, Hume and Green share the conviction that human practice is guided by pre-existing mental settings. Hume's belief that human knowledge is framed by pre-existing impressions and habits represents an early stage of transcendental thinking. In retrospect, we can say that Hume discovered the transcendental function of the 'world of passions', which, as we shall see, is very similar to what in Green's terminology would be called a 'world of spirit'.

1.1   Defining the term 'transcendental'

In his review of Watson's book on Kant, Green comments that with respect to Kant every critic faces the choice of either punctiliously revealing what the German idealist explicitly stated and believed, or of bringing out unarticulated yet significant messages with which his philosophy was 'pregnant':

It comes to be a question of the extent and direction in which we are to 'develop his meaning'; whether we are to understand him according to the letter of statements which he undoubtedly makes, but which we may be inclined to regard as survivals of a way of thinking which it was the true result of his philosophy to set aside, or according to what may seem to us the spirit of his more pregnant passages.[2]

What Green says of Kant is true of himself. His philosophy contains insights which surpass what he would maintain to be his position. Green would proclaim himself to be an exponent of a belief in an objective Spirit, while his philosophy practically asserts the primary function of human subjectivity; he would think of himself as a defender of 'Reason',[3] while arguing convincingly that there is nothing like pure thought, undetermined by 'desire'.[4] The deeper we delve into Green's philosophy, the clearer it becomes that he is not speaking about an objective spirit – and it is on this assumption that he is qualified as an absolute idealist – but about a 'spiritual principle'. I shall argue that Green's philosophy contains transcendental arguments. His spiritual principle in fact represents a form of transcendental explanation of human practice. I use the term 'transcendental' as distinct from 'transcendent' – a distinction established by Immanuel Kant.[5]

For Kant transcendental philosophy is 'the system of all principles of pure reason'.[6] He applies the term 'transcendental' to 'this mode of knowledge [which] is possible *a priori*'.[7] Kant believes that 'though all knowledge begins with experience, it by no means follows that it arises out of experience'.[8] We acquire knowledge because we have the faculty of knowing. Our knowledge is conditioned by the preliminary work of the human mind: 'reason is the faculty which furnishes us with the principles of knowledge *a priori*'.[9] Kant's transcendental philosophy views experience as preconditioned by a set of pure *a priori* categories.

Kant, however, limits the sphere of transcendental philosophy to the field of speculative knowledge and 'experience' understood as 'empirical knowledge'.[10] He believes transcendental philosophy cannot be extended to an analysis of morals because 'all that is practical, so far as it contains motives, relates to feelings; and these belong to the empirical sources of knowledge'.[11]

However, Kant's transcendentalism can be applied with equal force in the field of morals or practical reason. Just as what we learn is preconditioned by our transcendental 'faculty of knowledge',[12] so what we do in general is preconditioned by the transcendental faculties of desiring, willing and thinking. All our experience, not only that concerning speculative knowledge, is made possible by the transcendental function of human reason. We find the same idea in Ernst Cassirer (1874–1945) in his introduction to *The Philosophy of Symbolic Forms* and in his *Essay on Man*: 'Kant's observation that for the human understanding it is both necessary and indispensable to distinguish between reality and possibility of things expresses not only a general characteristic of theoretical reason but a truth about practical reason as well.'[13] Cassirer believes that the real nature and full force of Kant's transcendental philosophy 'become even more evident if we turn to the development of our *ethical ideas and ideals*'.[14]

Transcendental philosophy investigates the conditions of human experience, that is, what makes this experience possible. Kant tries to identify all those formal concepts, rules and principles that determine the structure of knowledge. He believes these concepts, rules and principles have to be 'pure' – free from any experience themselves in order to be 'formal', 'universal' and 'objective'. That is why he is so determined not to admit anything 'empirical' to the sphere of the 'transcendental'. It is only pure thought that can have a transcendental function. While Kant limits the sphere of what preconditions experience to a set of purely rational categories, later transcendentalists including Edmund Husserl refer to structures of human consciousness in general. Husserl uses the term 'transcendental' to represent the philosophy that enquires into 'the ultimate source of all the formations of knowledge', into 'the ontic meaning of the pregiven life-world', and into 'the subjectivity which *ultimately* brings about all world-validity'.[15]

The transcendental idea in its full potential can be seen in the following terms. Our experience is formally preconditioned by the structure of human consciousness, by the way in which human faculties function. Transcendental philosophy aims at discovering those principles and concepts that serve as a foundation of everything we do or are capable of doing. Human experience is always preconditioned by a set of beliefs and ideas. Whence and how these beliefs and ideas are arrived at are issues that have divided different transcendentalists. The transcendental idea has progressed from asserting firmly fixed and pre-experiential transcendental categories (of the Kantian type) to discovering the dynamic and experience-dependent nature of transcendental concepts. An advanced version of transcendentalism can admit that the ideas and beliefs which pre-condition one's experience are also derived from experience. The core of the transcendental message is that in each particular moment, our experience is preconditioned – that is, made possible – by the conceptual baggage that has accumulated and is always present at the back of our minds – whether we are aware of it or not. I claim that Green is an exponent of the transcendental idea in its 'pregnant sense'. His philosophy stands somewhere between Kant and the form of transcendentalism I have just described.

The discovery of transcendental themes within Green's philosophy has been hindered by several factors, some of which are unconnected to Green himself. Among the former is the fact that current Anglo-American philosophy is little interested in the developments of Kantian transcendentalism and, accordingly, does not emphasise the distinctive character of the transcendental idea. The difference between 'transcendental' and 'transcendent' is seen as relevant only with respect to Kant, rather than in general.[16] Among the factors which have hindered a 'transcendental' interpretation of Green, and which are related to Green himself, I will consider two. First, the orig-inality of Green's philosophy had surpassed what he was prepared to maintain as his view. There are ideas implied in his arguments which none the less, Green would not openly profess. As I have mentioned, he would think of himself as an objective idealist and would not say that the 'spiritual principle' can be understood as the principle on which personal experience functions. His commitment to opposing naturalism would not permit him to admit that something of a non-rational nature could play a fundamental role in human motivation. This is clearly the main weakness of his epistemology, which I con-sider to be the second factor which hinders readers from finding Green's philosophy significant today. Green's philosophy has no greater enemy than his own epistemology, to which I now turn.

1.2   Green's metaphysics of knowledge

In his epistemology Green inherits mistakes first made by Kant. The German idealist's sharp opposition between transcendental categories and human experience (between *a priori* and *a posteriori*) resulted in the blurring of the distinction between experience and nature, both of which stood equally under what is *a posteriori*. In the context of Kant's epistemology, experience is related to phenomena and implies the use of the (inner or outer) senses, as opposed to the categories of understanding which are 'pure'. Experience is taken to comprise human interaction with nature. So experience and nature are seen as belonging to the sphere of what is non-purely rational. The Kantian discovery that experience is preconditioned by the categories of understanding was smoothly transferred from experience to nature. '[U]nderstanding makes nature' – Green quotes Kant in the first pages of his *Prolegomena*.[17] Kant's *Critique of Pure Reason* obliterates at times the distinction between human experience of nature and nature itself. Because nature was seen to be related to sense perception, it was taken to be the case that understanding participated not only in the synthesis of sense data, but also in the formation of what nature is. Although Kant was cautious to distinguish between phenomena and things in themselves (between nature as experienced by us and nature in itself), Green considered this distinction to be invalid.

Green's attitude with respect to the independent existence of nature was controversial. On the one hand he claimed that his idealism differed from the belief that 'the realities of the world' were identical with 'the feelings of men'.[18] Green thought that it was an 'absurdity' to claim 'that nature comes into existence in the process by which this person or that begins to think'.[19] He contended that this belief was counter-intuitive and he did not share it. On the other hand, he argued that 'we can attach no meaning to "reality", as applied to the world of phenomena, but that of existence under definite and unalterable relations; and we find that it is only for a thinking consciousness that such relations can subsist.'[20] It is this second line of thought, expressing a stronger idealist position, which creates problems for Green's philosophy.[21] Although his sympathetic critics place more emphasis on the first side of his idealism – its milder form – I believe that it is important to explain why Green was led to maintain the second one. The latter cannot easily be overlooked as it comes across very strongly in Book I of his *Prolegomena*, which aims to outline the metaphysical foundation of his ethical theory. I shall deal with this in more detail below.

I will consider three problematic elements with respect to the 'absolutist' version of Green's idealism, and, accordingly, with respect to his epistemology as a whole: the eternal consciousness; Green's theory of relations; and the failure (inherited from Kant), to distinguish between experience and nature. I will review these in turn.

While Green's eternal consciousness can be dispensed with in his milder, idealist outlook, it is a necessary component of the stronger one. So long as Green believes that the formative function of thought applies only to human experience, we can easily reinterpret his 'eternal consciousness' as 'the general structure of human consciousness'. Colin Tyler argues that this 'infamous concept can be depersonified and hence becomes the underlying structure of human consciousness'.[22] However, so long as Green claims that the unity of the world is pre-given by a 'self-distinguishing consciousness', that 'consciousness ... constitutes reality and makes the world one', the introduction of an extra-human consciousness becomes a necessary step.[23] Clearly, the unity of nature cannot be pre-given by any single mind: if it is to be pre-given by a spiritual principle – as Green claims it is – then this spiritual principle must have an 'objective', extra-human existence. The eternal consciousness that holds the 'unalterable relations' which give unity to nature is an agency that transcends any personal consciousness and thus differs from it. This kind of spiritual principle cannot be reinterpreted in the sense of 'the general structures of human consciousness' as it has to be extra-human. In this form, Green's epistemology is difficult to accept.

Green's path towards asserting the existence of the eternal consciousness has been paved by his flawed concept of 'relations'. Ironically enough, Green inherited his concept from Locke, whose empiricism he criticised extensively. 'It might seem strange [Anthony Quinton points out] that one of traditional empiricism's most insistent and unrelenting critics should attribute so much authority to a most conspicuous empiricist.'[24] Locke believes that our feelings reflect data coming from outside, while our thought produces the relations into which our sense data are organised. Green never contests that. His criticism of Locke consists in reversing the order in which human knowledge is accrued: it is not that we receive sensations and then put them together in thought, but vice versa. We are able to perceive things only because we already have an apparatus of categories which unites all sense data in a meaningful presentation. Green's mistake was to believe that while all sensations come from 'outside', all relations come from 'inside' – from thought. John Skorupski clearly shows the weakness of this position:

> Even if Locke thinks relations to be the work of the mind, or Berkeley considers them 'neither a feeling nor felt',[25] why cannot a new empiricist accept that ideas of relation are derived from experience? Can it not be given in experience that this shade is bluer than that? That this edge is longer than that?[26]

Things in the external world are already related in one way or another and we perceive these relations in the same way in which we perceive the related objects. The formative function of human consciousness consists in our ability to obtain meaningful information from the external environment. It synthesises the data we receive and creates a coherent unity of our experience, yet it does not produce all the relations between things.

The problem with Green's concept of relations comes from his failure to account for the distinction between nature and experience. He is right to advance the idea that facts are relations in the sense that in order to register even the simplest fact one relies on the preliminary concepts one's consciousness contains. However, this applies to facts as registered by human beings, as belonging to human experience. Every piece of coherent experience relies on a preliminary act of thought. This is not the case about those things that do not belong to human experience.

The critique of Green's theory of relations brings us to a number of complicated issues of transcendentalism which Green touches on in Book I, but does not resolve. Do all transcendental functions belong to pure thought? Green's concept of relations is firmly tied to the work of thought – relations always come from a 'thinking consciousness', from a 'combining intelligence'.[27] Even with the qualification that Green's concept of relations is applicable only in the realm of human experience, there remains the question, how precise is this concept? Should the work of the consciousness which preconditions every simple piece of experience be identified exclusively with 'relations', or the work of thought? The fact that

Kant defines his transcendental categories of understanding in terms of 'pure thought' is a weakness in his transcendentalism – a weakness that Green overcomes in his theory of the will, yet inherits in his metaphysics of knowledge.

Let me explain why Green's concept of relations is inadequate even if applied to the sphere of experience. The problem is that Green relies heavily on a distinction – between thought and feelings – which he later tries to obliterate. As a result, his concept of relations becomes untenable. Green needs this distinction because he builds his new brand of idealism on it. This distinction is similar to Kant's sharp opposition between the pure categories of understanding and the empirical employment of the human faculties, that is, between the *a priori* and *a posteriori*. This distinction is used by the two philosophers as a means to avoid subjective idealism of Berkeley's type which professes that things exist only so long as they are perceived. Green believes that by arguing that facts are not feelings but relations (that is, given by the work of mind) he dissociates himself from the idealism that denies the existence of all things beyond human experience. He says that 'the idealism which interprets facts as relations, and can only understand relations as constituted by a single spiritual principle, is chargeable with no such outrage on common-sense'.[28] We can see that Green relies on his theory of relations for the purpose of proving that his idealism is of a different kind from the one which claims that there are no facts apart from our perceptions of them. So on the one hand, the distinction between relations and feelings is important because on its basis Green qualifies his own type of idealism. On the other hand, he negates this distinction by claiming that there is nothing like 'mere feeling' undetermined by the relations coming from a self-distinguishing consciousness.[29] First, he overpowers his concept of relations and thus 'forces' his theory towards the absolute idealism of the eternal consciousness. As a clear demarcation between facts and relations is almost impossible, to claim that all relations come from the mind is also to claim that everything comes from the mind. Secondly, he argues that not only is there nothing like mere feeling, but also that there is nothing like mere thought. He rejects the distinction as invalid. Peter Hylton observes that this amounts to a 'complete surrender of the idea that the world is constituted by thought. If thought is correlative with feeling, and is an abstraction from experience, it surely cannot constitute experience.'[30] As Green's concept of relation is too closely linked with 'thought', the ambiguities about the nature and function of thought make this concept untenable. No wonder it has no important use in Green's theories of general and moral practice. Unfortunately, it holds a central position in his epistemology and in his extensive criticism of Hume's philosophy.

1.3   Hume's discovery of the 'world of spirit'

The distinction between thought and feelings lays the foundations for Green's relation theory, yet he goes on to argue that there is no mere feeling or thought unrelated to each other. In his theory of the will Green explains at length that over-emphasising this distinction has led to serious misconceptions with respect to the work of the human spirit. I fully embrace this line of his philosophy and I make a point of underlining its advantages.

There is an important distinction, however, which is central to Green's entire philosophical enterprise of explaining the spiritual principle. Although I criticise Green's opposition of feelings and thought (as well as Kant's distinction between experience and the pure work of thought), I believe that another distinction – that between the world of human experience and non-human nature – is vital to the delivery of his philosophical message. Green's task is to rescue the science of ethics from the naturalists. He needs to prove that human experience functions on a different principle from everything else that belongs to non-human nature. The idea of the 'spiritual principle' is founded on its contrast to a 'natural principle' and this contrast should be kept alive, not mitigated. Green never loses his intuition that this distinction has to be made, yet his philosophy is ambiguous as to where exactly the dividing line should be drawn. It is Green's weakness to believe that thought belongs to spirit, while feelings belong to nature. It is his strength to believe that within human beings thoughts and feelings are inextricably linked and human experience in its totality belongs to the sphere of spirit. In his theory of the will the second message plays a fundamental role. However, in his epistemology it has only a nominal presence. Green's vacillation between these two beliefs does not allow him to appreciate fully an important discovery contained in the philosophy of David Hume.

Green was the first English philosopher to produce a long and in depth analysis of Hume's *Treatise of Human Nature*. He wrote extensive introductions to the two volumes of the *Treatise*, published in 1874.[31] For Green, 'Hume's great genius lay in the rigour with which he argue[d] from Locke's fundamental principles, resolutely ignoring common sense, and arriving at absurdity. For empiricist philosophers after Hume, Green has very little respect, for he sees in their work a series of attempts to evade or disguise the bankruptcy of Empiricism which Hume had demonstrated.'[32] Green accuses Hume of failing to understand the work of thought in the process of perception. What Hume counts as a feeling (Green refers to Hume's use of 'identity'), Green argues is a relation, 'and relations, as Green is never tired of saying, are the work of thought'.[33] Green's criticism of Hume, although deemed unfounded by Norman Kemp Smith, is still considered valid in many ways.[34] However, as it is of little help in my current purpose of emphasising a particularly strong aspect of Hume's philosophy, I shall not analyse it here.

In this section I will offer a short analysis of Hume's *Treatise*.[35] This will reveal that Hume develops views coherent with the deepest meaning of Green's philosophy. Hume contributes to a purpose which was inherently Green's – he reveals that any attempt to present a simple picture of human mentality is bound to produce false results. Green's idea that 'mere thought' does not exist could not have found a more passionate exponent than Hume in his critique of reason. Green's conviction that human experience is predetermined by a preliminary work of consciousness is practically exemplified by Hume's observations that people's certainty in knowledge is underpinned by already existing preconceptions and beliefs. Green was not in a position to analyse his own philosophy in the terms I am analysing it – terms I have borrowed from developments in continental philosophy subsequent to Green. This also explains why he could not interpret Hume's philosophy along the line suggested in this section.

David Carr points out that 'Hume was for Husserl the more radical [compared to Kant] transcendental philosopher' because 'Kant's transcendentalism did not penetrate to the role of the pre-given life-world in subjective life.'[36] Husserl recognises Hume as the forefather of transcendentalism. For although Hume himself did not reach the philosophical conclusions made by Kant and

Husserl, his philosophy contains transcendental ideas. In critiquing his philosophy we can say that Hume discovered the transcendental function of the 'world of passions', which, as we shall see, is very similar to what in Green's terminology would be called a 'world of spirit'.

In the conclusion to Book I of his *Treatise* Hume writes: 'Human Nature is the only science of man; and yet has been hitherto the most neglected.'[37] Because philosophers have failed to appreciate the power of habit, custom and propensities on human knowledge, they have made false metaphysical assertions. They have failed to see the impossibility of certain and objective knowledge. What philosophers have believed to be rational and thus true – such as, the firmness of the relation between cause and effect – is actually only an assumption underpinned by belief, vivacity of impressions and habit. Hume endeavours to show that knowledge is not a straightforward phenomenon of perception and rational assessment but, on the contrary, it is a process heavily obstructed by a 'belt' of attitudes, dispositions, ambitions and dreams. This revelation provokes Hume's sorrow and epistemological despair.[38] What people have believed to be the truth of the external world, Hume now discovers to be lying 'merely in ourselves'. The firm knowledge of the facts and laws of nature proves to be a covert expression of our personal determination, thirst for knowledge and disposition to believe. Philosophy and science turn out to be less related to the actual state of events than to human purposes and cravings: 'If we believe, that fire warms, or water refreshes, 'tis only because it costs us too much pains to think otherwise.'[39] Most of us believe that Hume is mistaken to claim that the causal link necessarily belongs to the human mind rather than to the interlinked events themselves. Certain events are related causally, independently of all subjective attitudes. However, Hume has made an important discovery with tremendous philosophical consequences. His message extends beyond the claim that we can never prove the causal link between two events.

Hume's contribution to the analysis of human nature consists in uncovering a range of psychological phenomena that comprise a world of their own. He dispenses with the simplistic notion of human mentality as a dichotomy between the senses and reason, or between emotions and reason. Hume's intention to prove that reason is neither the crowning faculty nor the core of human nature is not realised in terms of playing up the importance of basic human instincts. When Hume argues that reason is not the sole governing voice in epistemology or morals, the core of his argument is that human nature is too complex to be guided by it. It is not the strength of our basic instincts, but the intricacy of our emotional world that Hume emphasises. His attack on reason is not at the expense of a poor picture of the human psyche. On the contrary, he pioneers a philosophical analysis of the 'world of spirit'. Nothing in the world of non-human nature parallels the phenomena of the human spirit. The latter is a labyrinth of passions and aspirations and to believe that human reason can ignore or overrule it is the greatest naivety of antecedent philosophy. Hume wants to draw philosophers' attention to a problem that has not previously been acknowledged: the density, and the insurmountability, of the world of passions. This is the world which would subsequently be investigated by the German and the British idealists; Green would do much to clarify its nature.

Hume and Green would disagree on the role reason plays in the world of passions. Hume is clearly determined to keep reason separate from anything that can fundamentally explain human behaviour. Hume's rejection of reason is, in a sense, ideological. This rejection is pursued with a notable determination to ignore the obvious ways in which reason is involved in human desire for knowledge or moral action.[40] However, Hume's determination to play down the importance of reason is triggered by a very worthwhile aim: to uncover the range of faculties and factors which constitute mental life. The scale and the variety of this range have usually been hidden behind simplistic concepts of reason. By identifying the entire mental sphere with 'thinking', philosophers have 'collapsed' human spirituality into a single faculty. Thus, by rejecting reason, Hume is tearing down a curtain of concealment. The variety of factors that determine our thinking has never been properly assessed. Although many philosophers have given due acknowledgement to the existence and power of human emotion, the particular philosophical assessment of the extent to which it penetrates our 'scientific' or 'impartial' thinking is Hume's. If Hume is sceptical about the possibility of human knowledge, it is because he believes that we cannot rise above our passions and ignore them by thought, because thought itself is guided by aspirations.

Book III of the *Treatise*, entitled 'Of Morals', gives us a fuller picture of Hume's concept of human nature. In Book III it is apparent that recourse to feelings as the basis of all moral phenomena does not cause as much anguish as it did in Book I, 'On the Understanding'. The world of human emotions was seen as a blinding, opaque belt obstructing the 'vision' of human knowledge, but the same world is the legitimate sphere of morals. Hume speaks of morals as a special field, not only independent of reason, but also essentially different from all other phenomena in nature.[41] When he explains why morality is not based on reason, he simultaneously does two things. On the one hand, he indirectly shows how previous philosophers have failed to understand human experience: Hume's criticism of reason is in essence a criticism of the philosophical and scientific methodologies formerly applied to the study of human nature. On the other hand, he gives a richer description of the nature of the spiritual world by claiming that it is 'active'.

Let me review these in turn.

Hume can justifiably be accused of giving too simple an account of the work of reason. It is only on the basis of this inadequate account that he can so easily dismiss the role of reason in moral behaviour. He says: '... the operations of human understanding divide themselves into two kinds, the comparing of ideas, and the inferring of matter of fact.'[42] Further, he argues that if morality can be analysed with the tools of this understanding, it has to be subsumed under four types of rational relations, which are '*[r]esemblance, contrariety, degrees in quality*, and *proportions in quantity and number*'.[43] He concludes his argument by saying that morality is not susceptible to these relations. What we can see is that Hume's concept of reason is limited to the manner in which reason has been used or understood by mathematical science. We can argue that Hume's account of reason is neither accurate nor exhaustive.

What I find more interesting is the similarity between Hume's critique of reason and Green's critique of natural science.[44] The weakness of reason, according to Hume, is its inability to assess anything different from what it has been used to assess, namely, 'matters of fact' and 'inanimate' objects. In so far as moral life is constituted of 'actions, passions and volitions'[45] and these differ from inanimate matters of fact, reason is impotent in its attempts to analyse them.

Clearly, when speaking of reason, Hume means the ways reason has been employed by mathematical sciences, or by philosophers who have been guided in their research by the premises of these sciences. Let us consider the following quote:

> Reason is the discovery of truth or falsehood. Truth or falsehood consists in an agreement or disagreement either to the *real* relations of ideas, or to *real* existence and matter of fact. Whatever, therefore, is not susceptible of this agreement or disagreement, is incapable of being true or false, and can never be an object of our reason. Now 'tis evident our passions, volitions, and actions, are not susceptible of any such agreement or disagreement; being original facts and realities, complete in themselves, and implying no reference to other passions, volitions, and actions. 'Tis impossible, therefore, they can be pronounced either true or false, and be either contrary or conformable to reason.[46]

Hume's idea is that 'passions, volitions and actions' cannot be true or false because they do not belong to the world of nature about which the sciences had already built a system of categories. True and false are adjectives that can be applied only to those states of affairs about which we have a criterion for assessment and a detached standpoint. Morals, according to Hume, do not belong to those. First, they differ from everything belonging to non-human nature, and secondly, reason cannot take a detached stance towards them. '[M]orality consists not in any relations, that are the objects of science,' he argues.[47]

Hume's criticism of reason is at the same time a challenge to the empiricists' (Hobbes' and Locke's) understanding of reason. The empiricists fail to give a unified picture of human mentality. The individual is divided between natural impulses and thought. It is only thought that gives people their 'human character'. A vast amount of the human psyche is omitted – it is seen as belonging to nature in general – and only a small part of it, namely reason, crosses the boundary of what belongs particularly to human nature – human nature in its elevated sense. Hume points out that there are many faculties that belong to human nature. Although he excludes reason from them, he actually *expands* the notion of human nature.

Hume's critique of reason gives us a positive idea about the character of morals and, thereby, about the world of spirit. He writes:

> ... as reason can never immediately prevent or produce any action by contradicting or approving of it, it cannot be the source of the distinction betwixt moral good and evil, which are found to have that influence. Actions may be laudable or blameable; but they cannot be reasonable or unreasonable: Laudable or blameable, therefore, are not the same with reasonable or unreasonable. The merit or demerit of actions frequently contradict, and sometimes control our natural propensities. But reason has no such influence. Moral distinctions, therefore, are not the offspring of reason. Reason is wholly inactive, and can never be the source of so active a principle as conscience, or a sense of morals.[48]

Hume argues that, apart from reason, all the rest of human consciousness is an 'active principle'. It generates feelings, attitudes, actions and volitions. The claim that the moral sense is an active principle, while reason is wholly inactive, means also that human consciousness is greater than reason. Consciousness is a 'universe' of action, while reason is an impotent, single and isolated capacity.

Green disagrees with Hume. He asserts that 'the philosophy that makes "reason the slave of passion" cannot ... supply any effective defence of established manners against the wilfulness of the self-conscious sentiment.'[49] He believes that Hume's philosophy prepared the grounds for utilitarianism, which became widely popular in nineteenth-century England. Thus Hume set the future of English moral philosophy on the wrong path, leaving 'a theoretic age like ours' without 'a theory of [man's] own greatness'.[50]

However, there are several important aspects to Hume's philosophy which cohere in principle with Green's ideas in *Prolegomena*. Let me summarise them:

- human consciousness as a whole is different from non-human nature; it functions on different principles;
- when Hume speaks of human passions, he refers to a united whole; whether he calls it consciousness or morals, he refers to a 'set-up' or a 'structure' of related phenomena; Hume rejects the

importance of reason through counterpoising it to the world of passions; by playing down reason he plays up the complex phenomenon of human consciousness;

- the logic along which passions are interconnected is non-transparent to scientific thinking;
- Hume's attack on reason is also an attack against the practice of empirical science and against the impoverished image of human mentality inherent in empiricist thinking.

There are several reasons why Green fails to see the substantive character of the grounds he shares with Hume. First, as I have mentioned, Green is ambiguous about where the dividing line between human spirit and non-spiritual nature lies. In his epistemology he separates thought from feelings, while in his theory of the will he claims that human experience as a whole represents the work of the 'spiritual principle'. The ground where Green develops his criticism of Hume is his epistemological theory and it does not represent Green's philosophy in its entirety. What is more, this ground contradicts his theory of the will, which is where, I believe, Green's philosophical strength lies.

Secondly, Green was not in a position to assess the extent to which his ideas converged with Hume's as he took for granted some of the issues on which they agreed. Green could not see how someone might reject the view that any knowledge of morals and politics should be preceded by research into human nature. It was not until the twentieth century that political theorists would denounce metaphysics and, indeed, any in-depth analysis of human psychology. Today we can appreciate better what united and what distinguished Green and Hume. We are also in a better position to judge the scale of their common ground as we know the trends in political thought which reject assumptions held by both philosophers.

I cannot end this section without pointing out that credit has to be given to Green's criticism of Hume. The way Hume saw his own philosophy and the way in which it grew to be the 'popular philosophy' of nineteenth-century England differ from the interpretation offered hitherto. In support of Green's criticism, I will mention that first, Hume's understanding of the interaction between reason and the passions is too one-sided. However well Hume describes the process by which the passions penetrate the work of thought, he remains unaware of the way reason participates in constituting the passions. Secondly, Hume's analysis of morals lacks the depth and sophistication which Green finds in the human spirit. To explain virtue and vice on the basis of the dichotomy between pleasure and pain for Green is among the greatest fallacies of naturalist ethics.[51]

1.4   The spiritual principle that underpins human practice, or Green's theory of the will

Green develops his theory of human practice in Book II of *Prolegomena*, entitled 'The Will'. Hereafter I shall use the terms 'theory of the will' and 'theory of practice' interchangeably. Similarly the terms 'general human behaviour', 'general practice' or the expression Green himself uses, 'the world of practice', will be used synonymously.[52] By describing the mechanism of human practice, Green is explaining the nature of the spiritual principle. It is in the theory of the will that Green's philosophical originality begins to be clearly exhibited. Green introduces a principle by which human practice functions. This is expressed in two statements: first, that in all his desires a man pursues an idea or a concept; second that in all his desires a man is an object to himself. The principle of human practice has both a 'self-distinguishing' and 'self-seeking' character. These two aspects unite in one rule: in all acts of will 'a self-conscious individual directs himself to the realisation of some idea, as to an object in which for the time he seeks self-satisfaction'.[53] The rule will be easier to understand if we review its two aspects in turn.

Green claims that every desire is motivated by a concept. The object of desire does not consist in any particular item we are trying to obtain, but in *the idea* of ourselves having obtained that item. As conscious agents we are always motivated by an image, by an expectation which is present in the form of a concept. Only instinctive actions are not motivated by such a concept. 'By an instinctive action we mean one *not* determined by a conception, on the part of the agent, of any good to be gained or evil to be avoided by the action.'[54] Green believes that the scope of instinctive actions in practical life is negligible. Desires which are considered basic, such as the desire for food and shelter, also operate through the medium of a concept.

I will give an example in support of Green's assertion. When we are about to eat there are several factors, apart from hunger, that motivate us. We know that food satisfies hunger, we know that eating is necessary and good, and we can think of no reason why we should not eat this particular food at this moment. When I eat, I know that I am eating and I have an attitude towards myself in doing so: I know that I have to eat, or I hate myself for doing so, and so on.

The fact that desires are motivated by concepts implies that the agent *distinguishes* himself from each particular desire. The idea about the 'self-distinguishing' character of human consciousness is central to Green's philosophy. Human beings are always conscious of themselves as authors of their actions: whatever they are doing, they know they are doing it. When I drink a glass of water, I am conscious of myself drinking, I have let myself drink. In Green's words, the 'subject ... is ... related to the particular feelings, desires, and thoughts, which it thus distinguishes from and relate[s] to itself.'[55] This distinction puts the agent in a particular kind of control, not in the sense of deciding what to desire, but in the sense of being aware of that desire.

By claiming that human beings are motivated by 'concept', Green is arguing that human action is not guided by impulse. An agent can distance himself from his urges and from the circumstances surrounding his action. Through this distancing he is prevented from 'coinciding' with his impulses. Thus, what a person is does not collapse into a single urge. Each drive is only one of many. The human agent is always something more than each particular impulse; what she is supervenes upon it. This capacity of self-distancing prevents any single drive or factor from determining fully a person's practical life. This is the meaning behind Green's claim that the human being is a 'spiritual self-distinguishing subject'.[56]

To explain this theory, Green refers to and analyses the Old Testament story of Jacob and Esau.[57]

Jacob and Esau were twins, the sons of Isaac and Rebecca. Esau was the firstborn and so inherited the birthright. He liked hunting and spending time in the fields. Jacob was the opposite: he was quiet and stayed around the tents:

> One day Jacob was cooking some stew when Esau returned home completely tired out from hunting. He said to Jacob, 'Feed me, please, some of that red stuff. I'm about to faint.'

'Sell me your birthright,' Jacob replied, thinking quickly. ... This meant that when his father died, he got twice as much of his family wealth as any of his brothers. It also meant that his family would respect his opinion and accept his leadership. ...

Esau agreed. Then Jacob gave Esau some bread and the lentil stew.[58]

On the surface, this story about Esau who exchanged his birthright for a pot of lentil stew can be taken as an example of how someone can be guided by a thoughtless choice or by an animal urge. However, this case illustrates well the work of consciousness that Green is attempting to explain. Each object of desire is in itself a choice, and no choice is 'thoughtless'. Human beings do not seek to attain anything for its own sake: in attaining an object they seek a state of self-satisfaction. Choosing one object rather than another is also an act of establishing a priority. However strong an impulse is, and to whatever extent one surrenders to it, one is aware of a cost. Esau knew the cost of taking the food. Although the story implies that he was a little stupid, and that at the time he did not realise the consequences of his act,[59] Esau was aware of an alternative and he made a decision. When later he realised the consequences of his choice, he would *feel guilty* about what he had done. This capacity of being 'self-detached' is what makes Esau a morally imputable agent:

Since, however, it is not the hunger as a natural force, but his own conception of himself, as finding for the time his greatest good in the satisfaction of hunger, that determines the act, Esau recognises himself as the author of the act. He imputes it to himself, and it is morally imputable to him – an act for which he is accountable, to which praise or blame are appropriate.[60]

It is one of Green's beliefs that human beings have the capacity to overcome the force of circumstances. This, however, is not the essence of the principle of human practice which he is trying to explain. Green does not say that what determines our desires is our explicit decision. None the less, our actions are guided by an 'idea'. Our desires are not determined by circumstances, but by an idea which unites or 'interprets' these circumstances in a meaningful way. The coherence of one's behaviour is predetermined by the 'singleness' of one's self. All particular feelings, desires and thoughts are united by a single self-consciousness. They have no independent existence as factors of one's motivation or behaviour. Taken apart from the individual they are abstractions:

> If we are told that the Ego or self is an abstraction from the facts of our inner experience – something which we 'accustom ourselves to suppose' as a basis or substratum for these, but which exists only logically, not really,[61] – it is a fair rejoinder, that these so-called facts, our particular feelings, desires, and thoughts, are abstractions, if considered otherwise than as united in the character of an agent who is an object to himself.[62]

Human experience is always 'synthesised' by a single consciousness. Different factors and circumstances acquire meaning, or become motives for action, only if they are related to one's well-being. So, I never simply desire an object for its own sake. The objects I desire are part of my idea of my well-being: in every object I desire myself. In each desire an agent 'is an object to himself'.[63]

This takes us to the second aspect of Green's rule of practical behaviour: to the content of the concept that motivates human action. One's action is always motivated by some idea of *self-satisfaction*. Something becomes an object of desire because it contributes in some way to the well-being of the desiring agent. This is the meaning behind Green's abstract statement that in his desires an agent is always 'an object to himself'. Human action is motivated by 'concepts' of one's well-being. Spontaneous urges or wants become motives of action only if they become part of someone's idea of what is good for him: '[a want] only becomes a motive, so far as upon the want there supervenes the presentation of the want by a self-conscious subject to himself, and with it the idea of a self-satisfaction to be attained in the filling of the want.'[64]

The second aspect of Green's rule of human practice – that in his acts the individual is an object to himself – adds to Green's definition of the spiritual principle. It is not only 'self-distinguishing', but also 'self-seeking'. Claiming that human practice is guided by a 'self-seeking' principle is another way of saying that in all his activities the individual pursues a state of self-satisfaction. The way in which our desires are motivated by an idea of our well-being forms a permanent pattern: it works as a principle. There is one important thing with respect to the work of the 'self-seeking' principle that has to be noted. In each desire we seek a *better* state of our own. We constantly project an idea of this better state into the future. Each desire is motivated by an image of the state of events we seek, but is not present at the moment. Thus human experience is a constant self-projection and a self-expansion. The principle by which experience becomes united is the seeking of a richer well-being, of a fuller self-unity.

This process of 'self-renewal' becomes the focal point of the world of practice. Everything else is relative to it because everything acquires its meaning only within this process:

> The difficulty of saying what this all-uniting, self-seeking, self-realising subject is – the 'mystery' that belongs to it – arises from its being the only thing, or a form of the only thing, that is real (so to speak) in its own right; the only thing of which the reality is not relative and derived.[65]

What undergirds every analysis of practical behaviour is the idea by which one's action has been motivated. As we shall see, the same intuition will be expressed in a number of other ways in the *Prolegomena*, and in Green's political theory.

I will briefly explain and defend Green's theory of practice by using a slightly different terminology. Human practice does not operate through following our instincts for the simple reason that we learn from experience. We are guided by our instincts together with what we know from having previously attempted to satisfy them. This changes everything. Storing experience takes place by conceptualising it: learning by experience means developing values that come with priorities. Each impulse becomes a motive of desire only through the media of these priorities. Thus all our actions, however simple, are mediated by concepts of synthesised experience. The principle of the synthesis is relatedness to one's well-being. Thus our pursuit of well-being functions *as a principle of unifying experience* rather than a selfish instinct. So, since in all our desires we are guided by a conception, and since this conception has been formed by relating all factors to one's well-being, in all our desires we are objects to ourselves.

1.5   Why Green's principle is in fact a transcendental rule

Green's second attempt to explain the mechanism of human practice takes place in his analysis of the general nature of the human faculties of desiring and understanding.[66] He argues that although desiring and understanding are different activities, they are always performed by a single agent and, more importantly, they work through a common mechanism. By describing their common mechanism, Green effectively enters a second definition of the principle of human practice, as follows: 'The element common to both [desiring and understanding] lies *in the consciousness of self and a world as in a sense opposed to each other, and in the conscious effort to overcome this opposition.*' Here Green appeals for the reader's patience while he explains 'those dark and lofty statements'.[67]

What Green calls 'an object of desire' is never the particular thing that is verbally named as wanted. If we want to read a book, listen to music or go to Athens, it is not the book, the music or Athens that is the object of our desire. Before these things become 'objects of desire', they are transformed. If we want to read a book, the object of desire is our experience of reading. In each desire we pursue a state of ourselves, different from the state we are presently in. So each desire reveals an awareness that what we want to be the case is not yet the case; an awareness of an opposition between what is and what could be. Each desire is an attempt to transcend an existing boundary. Each desire implies an effort to appropriate something from the external world into our internal world, to make something that is real in itself into something that is real for us. Green says that 'the desire is at once a consciousness of opposition between a man's self and the real world, and an effort to overcome it by giving a reality in the world, a reality under the conditions of fact, to the object which, as desired, exists merely in his consciousness.'[68] Each act of desiring can be seen, on analysis, to be a process of personal expansion, of expanding the inner human world into the external objective world.

The process of understanding, on analysis, is similar. When Green looks for 'the generic nature of thought' he finds that 'it is only for a self-conscious soul that the senses reveal facts or objects at all'.[69] We are able to perceive and to register phenomena from the external environment only by associating them with our pre-existing perceptions. Understanding is a process of incorporating whatever had been hitherto alien into a system of familiar objects. So again, as with desire, the generic nature of thinking presupposes an awareness of a discrete world and an effort to incorporate this world into our personal world.

What Green offers us here can be seen as an investigation into the *a priori* structure of human consciousness, and thus, as a transcendental analysis. Before I go further, I will explain what is valuable about transcendentalist approaches to investigating human behaviour.

I will distinguish between human nature theorists and transcendentalists, where Hobbes, Locke and Hume belong to the first category, and Kant, Green and Husserl to the second. Both categories of philosopher believe that human practice is *preconditioned* by the complicated character of human nature. There is something special about human nature, which unless investigated properly, will leave moral and political practice profoundly misunderstood. The difference between the two types of philosopher is that the natural theorists tend to reduce human nature to basic urges and impulses. They do not succeed in incorporating reason with the other human faculties in a coherent whole. Whatever allowance they give to the complex character of human passions, and even to the existence of secondary nature, they fail to unite all impulses and urges on the one side, and thought on the other, into a single system. The transcendentalists go one step further by identifying human nature with human consciousness: thus they get closer to presenting a principle which can give human nature a unitary character. So when they explain what *preconditions* human behaviour they do not try to trace a chain of causal links and find out which particular passion is the starting point. What they see as underpinning human behaviour is, rather, a system of factors, which we can attempt to formalise. Kant argues that human understanding contains *a priori* categories.

Kantian transcendentalism leaves a number of questions unanswered. It remains a puzzle where the transcendental categories of the understanding come from and how they can be absolutely 'pure' from experience. In his theory of the will Green does not speak about *a priori* categories (although he does in his epistemology). For he inherits Kantian transcendentalism not by its letter, but by its spirit. Kant's philosophy suggested that at the back of our minds, underlying our behaviour, processes take place that determine what we do. Green is very sensitive to this insight and clearly takes it further. He does not introduce pure categories of thought, but a principle, a formal structure of human action. He advances the idea that what predetermines general behaviour is a dynamic process of self-projection.

Let us return to Green's claim that at the core of desire and of understanding there exists an effort to penetrate the boundary between our inner world and the external environment. This is another way of stating that in all his desires an agent is an object to himself. A desire which is distinct from an impulse, Green claims, 'involves a consciousness of its object, which in turn involves a consciousness of self'.[70] What preconditions human behaviour is an awareness of the gap between an internal and external world and a desire to bridge that gap; an awareness of inner limits and a desire to extend them. We can understand this to be the transcendental scheme of human practice in general. *What preconditions human behaviour at each particular moment is an already accomplished process of projecting a concept of our well-being as an object of pursuit.*

Although Green explains his position without using the vocabulary of transcendentalism, I believe that using it to analyse his text achieves a double purpose. First, it helps to explain the shortcomings of the so-called human nature theorists and the advantages of Green's theory over theirs. Secondly, it places Green in a context and thus helps reveal his achievement.

The purpose of transcendentalism is to show that what preconditions human behaviour is a system of concepts, that is, something in the formation of which reason has participated. Human behaviour is preconditioned by a structure that has a rational content. What makes human practice possible is not a set of natural faculties but a system of rational contents. Green openly and articulately pursues the purpose of transcendental philosophy. He claims that human behaviour is guided by a 'spiritual principle'. Hume had successfully argued that human thought was predetermined: that certain processes, inaccessible to our awareness, took place prior to our conscious actions. What Green wanted to reveal, however, is that in the processes that take place prior to our conscious behaviour, reason also participates, albeit in a latent form. Green's and Hume's philosophies share the conviction that there is something that operates in the back of our minds, something that pulls the strings without our being fully aware of it. However, Green argues, this thing is not of a 'natural' but of a spiritual origin.

Green's theory of practice offers the skeleton of this advanced form of transcendentalism which I outlined at the beginning of this chapter. He reveals that what functions as an *a priori* determination of human behaviour is not a natural faculty, not a circumstance, nor a combination of these: it is a *process* through which all these factors are synthesised into a concept. Also important, he tells us, is that this synthesis is based on a principle. According to him this principle is the pursuit of one's well-being. The idea is that this synthesis follows a logical process. It is not a blind or a 'mindless' interaction of factors; it is a synthesis that has meaning. Factors and circumstances influence human behaviour only through a synthesis which, as performed by human consciousness, is never mindless. When Green argues that the preconditioning of human behaviour is 'rational', he advances a more complex notion of rationality. 'Rational' is not only what is a direct product of thought. Green means rational in the sense of 'related to a purpose', or 'traceable to a recognisable meaning' – rational as opposed to 'senseless' or random.

These insights are implied in Green's practical philosophy, but he would not necessarily have accepted this particular expression of them, had it been presented to him. As we shall see in Chapter 3, section 3.2, Green's common good theory reveals his ambiguity about whether moral attitudes are outcomes of *a process* or fixed traits of human nature. Green also remains ambivalent with respect to his understanding of the transcendental function of reason. On the one hand, he presents Reason (in a capitalised form) as a pure thought which preconditions experience by organising it in 'relations'.[71] On the other hand, he sees it in the sense just described: thought participates in the transcendental work of the human consciousness; our behaviour, however spontaneous, is never mindless, never 'thought-free'.

1.6   Applications of Green's transcendental rule

The latter aspect of thought becomes clearer if we follow Green's analysis of the intricate relation between 'understanding' and 'desire', between 'will' and 'desire', and between 'will' and 'intellect'.[72] I have already reviewed the link between understanding and desire where I introduced Green's transcendental rule. More becomes clear from Green's discussion of the link between the will and the intellect. In these passages of the *Prolegomena* Green presents an analysis of human mentality that has application in all philosophy relating to human action: in ethics, in political theory, in epistemology.

The discussion about the will and intellect presents Green's understanding of thought in a new light. By trying to prove Hume wrong, Green also implicitly rejects has own theory about 'relations'.[73] Green contests the widespread misconception that thought is a process 'running parallel' to other mental processes, that it is a discrete faculty for synthesising data.

Green gives as an example someone who argues that thinking about paying a debt does not amount to actually paying it. What Green disagrees with is that the thought falls far short of the action. To counter-argue this, Green claims that such a thing as mere thought does not exist. He says that the thought of paying a debt would not have occurred unless the agent had the particular problem of having borrowed money. His argument is that separate ideas do not form a thought unless they belong to a particular agent and unless they are related to other pre-existing ideas. Green compares the process of thinking to that of perceiving in the sense that both presuppose a single agent and an already existing system of perceptions and ideas to which the new ones can relate:

> Just as sensuous impressions are constantly occurring to us which tell us nothing, suggest nothing, because they do not fit into any context of ideas, so ideas are constantly, as we say, passing through our minds without forming part of any process of thought speculative or practical, as defined by reference to an end.[74]

Thinking is 'defined by reference to an end'. So thinking implies both a subject that performs it and a purpose with respect to which it is performed. The subject who wills is the same subject who thinks. The thought itself is a solution, or a possible solution of the problem carried out by the 'willing' person. Thinking does not occur as a parallel process to the process of feeling, desiring or willing. It is not a detached power of putting data together by means of fixed logical connections. The 'logic' of the synthesis performed by thinking is determined by the 'end' of one's action. Thinking is our capacity to synthesise, but the principle of the synthesis is laid down by the particular personal situation that needs resolution.

In Book I of the *Prolegomena*, 'Metaphysics of Knowledge', Green made a statement which appears very similar to his ideas on the relation between the will and the intellect. There he stated that pure thought and pure feelings do not exist as such. However, his argument there was different from the one we are discussing here. In Book I he claimed that '[t]hought has no function in it except as constantly co-ordinating ever new appearances in virtue of their presence to that one subject'.[75] Thought cannot be pure because its work shows only with respect to the appearances it places in 'relations' to each other. None the less, in the full context of Green's epistemological theory, thought is seen as *having priority over* feelings and appearances. As opposed to Hume, who believes that passions are active and thought passive, Green's metaphysics of knowledge implies that thought is the active agent which injects reality into the otherwise scattered and 'meaningless' feelings and appearances.

The 'will–intellect' discussion reveals a completely different conception of thought. The reason why thought cannot be pure is not that it simply needs the material on which only it can exercise its combining potential. Now Green shows that thinking *cannot* take place if isolated from a particular situation. Different ideas can cross one's mind, he says, yet none of them amounts to a thought unless related to an end. Ideas need to be united in order to produce a coherent thought. Thought will not occur if there is no particular problem to be resolved, or a desire to be satisfied. Will and desire participate in the constitution of thought. So the spiritual principle cannot be identified with thought. In the same vein, the work of human consciousness cannot be defined as the reason that yields all the relations.

None the less, thinking retains its transcendental function. It still preconditions experience. Now we can define this function with more precision. The transcendental role of reason consists in the fact that thinking is *implied* in all human activities – even those which, on the surface, seem to be 'thought-free'. Desire and will always imply either explicit or latent thinking. However, with respect to thought, desire and will play the same transcendental role. They are conditions for its possibility.

These discoveries pose questions about the entire transcendental project. Now we are in a better position to see why Green's intention to explain the work of consciousness through his epistemology was doomed to failure. Green's belief in the primary position of a metaphysics of knowledge with respect to a metaphysics of practice was conditioned by his belief in the primary position of thought with respect to human experience. Green presumed that thought was constitutive of feeling, knowledge constitutive of reality. This was disproved by his theory of the will. There he revealed how thought, will and desire each had a constitutive (transcendental) function in equal measure. This shows that a transcendental philosophy should not be founded on a theory of knowledge, but on a theory of practice. Knowledge does not predetermine practice; it is part of it. Thought is not the transcendental condition of reality, it is itself transcendentally conditioned. The research into the transcendental work of human consciousness should find its proper beginning in the field of general human practice. It is no accident that Green started his original transcendental analysis in his theory of the will.

1.7   The difference between transcendentalism and spiritual determinism

What I see as the transcendental aspect of Green's theory of practice Colin Tyler defines as 'spiritual determinism'.[76] I believe that Tyler and I are both trying to explain the same aspect of Green's philosophy, namely, Green's view that human behaviour is essentially predetermined by the mechanism in which human consciousness works. However, we give this aspect different 'names', and respectively, draw different conclusions. I will briefly present and comment on Tyler's view of Green's spiritual determinism.

Tyler suggests two possible ways in which Green's theory of the will can be interpreted – along neo-Aristotelian lines, and along 'spiritual determinist' theory lines. He believes that 'the philosophical case in favour' of the second is stronger.[77] Green's spiritual determinism is expressed in the philosopher's belief that 'all thought – necessarily including all objects of desire and all willing – requires and is fundamentally structured by the nature of the eternal consciousness as it has been made explicit as the particular consciousness of the particular individual'.[78] However, Tyler considers this belief to be non-commendable as it 'logically entail[s] jettisoning any commitment to ideas such as voluntary action, moral responsibility and even ethical action'.[79] In the context of this argument, Tyler fully embraces Sidgwick's charge against Green: that the British idealist has denied the possibility of an agent acting otherwise than she has done in given circumstances. Thus Green has deprived her of any moral responsibility.[80]

I disagree with Tyler's conclusion that Green's 'spiritual determinist' theory deprives the agent of the choice of her actions. His argument boils down to the claim that if a person is 'determined', no matter how, then she cannot be free. Let me examine Tyler's line of thought. He refers to Green's claim that an individual cannot decide what to will, because she is not something different from her will;[81] that thought does not work independently of will and desire, as the person who thinks is the same as the one who wills. Thus Tyler concludes that 'Green's theory rests on the assumption that, in Bosanquet's words, "all logical process without exception is unconscious"'; it is thus a matter of pure luck that 'the particular individual's history has lead to the development of a particular will'.[82]

Green does claim that there is no act undetermined by the spiritual nature of the agent, undetermined by the fact that in all her desires, a person is an object to herself. But it is this 'determination' that makes human experience possible; it is the very condition of rational and unified experience. This 'determinism' does not deprive the person of her 'agency': it *is* her agency. Green has it as his task to investigate the specific way in which the human spirit functions. The discovery that experience, at each moment, is preconditioned by the function of human consciousness and by the accumulated conceptual baggage, does not imply the impossibility of free agency; it *defines* the agency. The transcendental rule gives the format, the parameters of human behaviour. Within these parameters a person may or may not be an autonomous agent (this is discussed further in chaper 2). I believe that calling Green's theory of the will 'transcendental' rather than 'spiritual determinist' explains better what he aimed for and achieved.[83]

Sidgwick's charge that Green's moral theory eventually deprives the individual of his moral responsibility has grounds, yet not in Green's 'spiritual determinism'. It is Green's failure to establish a clear demarcation between his practical and his moral theory which poses threats to his interpretation of moral behaviour. This is the subject of the next chapter.

2
Green's Phenomenological Moral Theory

Contemporary critics see Green's moral philosophy as a reconciliation of opposing, one-sided ethical theories. Geoffrey Thomas
argues that 'Green offers a cogent alternative to the two standard
models of action explanation' – the belief-desire theory and the cog-
nitive model. Thomas also claims that Green 'presents a challenge
alike to Kantian and to utilitarian constructions of the traditional
scheme of motive, action, and consequence'.[1] David Weinstein
argues that Green's moral philosophy stands between 'Kantianism
and Consequentialism' as he 'combined a consequentialism of
moral self-realisation (of good will) with a vigorous defence of
strong moral rights'.[2] Avital Simhony discusses Green's 'relational
approach', which 'seeks to go beyond dichotomies by simultaneously rejecting the one-sidedness of each side of an opposition and
interrelating elements of both into a new perspective'.[3] I agree that
Green's moral philosophy stands between opposing views, but I
point out that this middle position is not unproblematic. Green
employs two perspectives in exploring morality and therefore he
gives not one, but two definitions of moral behaviour: a formal and
a substantive one. Because these two perspectives cannot easily be
reconciled, Green finds himself in difficulty when trying to give a
single, unitary and non-contradictory definition of the moral ideal.
He admits to 'moving in a circle'.[4] This chapter focuses on this circle
and takes it to be the philosophical core of Green's moral theory.

Green offers two definitions of moral behaviour. First, he defines
the moral act as an act performed out of 'good will', out of the
agents' 'imposition on themselves of rules requiring something to be

done irrespectively of any inclination to do it'.[5] This is the formal definition of moral action; Green also offers a substantive definition. The moral ideal is 'some type of man or character, or personal activity considered as an end in itself'.[6] These two definitions represent the two basic features of Green's 'system of Ethics': 'the distinction between the good and the bad will' and the affirmation of the unconditional value of human perfection.[7] The distinction between good and bad will is based on defining the nature of 'moral desire' as a desire for an object that is valuable in itself. This lays down the formal conditions of moral behaviour and can be taken as a sufficient definition of morality. However, Green does not leave open for specification the object of moral desire: he fills it with content by claiming that the true good is human perfection. Sections 2.2 and 2.3 will discuss the formal and substantive definitions in turn.

This dual defining of morality is not unproblematic. Green explains moral behaviour by means of two key concepts: the good will and the object that is good in itself. In his terminology these two key concepts are the good will and the unconditional good. So, on the one hand, he claims that an object of desire is morally good only if it is pursued with moral motivation, that is, with good will. On the other hand, he claims that there is an object that is truly good in itself and that an agent is a moral agent only if she pursues this moral good. This raises problems for his theory. How can there be an unconditional good, that is, a good that is not derived from the good will pursuing it? Green registers this difficulty when claiming that he is 'moving in a circle' in trying to define one by means of the other, and vice versa. I shall argue that acknowledging the existence of this circle marks an important theoretical step forward. In order to conceptualise Green's philosophical achievement, I characterise the circle as a 'phenomenological circle' (section 2.4). The existence of this circle can be explained by observing the change of perspective from which its two elements are defined (section 2.5). The phenomenological circle will prove to be a convenient tool for further assessment of Green's vision of the moral ideal, as well as of the common good, freedom and human rights, discussed respectively in Chapters 3, 4 and 5.

This chapter analyses Green's moral theory by disclosing one particular aspect that has received little attention so far: its phenomenological character. I argue that the strength of his moral philosophy is more apparent if its similarities to utilitarianism are more carefully explored (section 2.1). Green and the utilitarians have a very similar outlook on the general nature of human practice: both adopt a phenomenological perspective by defining the good through reference to individuals' desire. If Green had acknowledged this common ground, he would have been in a position to effect a reconciliation between his theory of human practice and his moral theory. Explaining moral behaviour goes hand in hand with addressing the difficult question of how one can pursue an object for its intrinsic worth when all human practice is guided by the pursuit of self-satisfaction. At the beginning of Book III of the *Prolegomena* Green poses this question directly.[8] However, in his critique of the utilitarians, Green disguises the problem. By denying the utilitarian claim that people pursue pleasure, he effectively dissociates himself from his own theory of human practice. Thus, he denies the validity of one side of the dilemma (that is, the view that human beings seek self-satisfaction) and associates his moral theory with the second side (that human beings pursue things for their intrinsic worth). Although he outlines the formal conditions of moral actions as pursuing an object in a self-disinterested manner, he fails to reconcile them with his transcendental rule, clearly and explicitly (see sections 1.4 and 1.5, above). My criticism of Green's critique of utilitarianism is to the benefit of his ethical theory. We shall see that Green's philosophy embraces both sides of the dilemma and with little additional reconstruction it can offer a resolution.

2.1 Similarities between Green and the utilitarians

In his theory of the will Green shows that the work of a self-objectifying consciousness preconditions human practice. The meaning of all objects of desire, of thought, of will is derived from their relation to a subject. The subject, in its turn, does not coincide with any of its pursued objects; it is always 'distinguished' from them; it poses them to itself. The objects of human experience are always related to, yet distinguished from, a subject. In Chapter 1, I argued that Green introduced a transcendental rule of human practice according to which in all her desires an agent is an object to herself; in all her desires she pursues an idea of self-satisfaction. In analysing Green's moral philosophy it is important to bear in mind the conclusions reached in his theory of human practice.

Green discloses his moral theory, in large measure, by criticising utilitarianism and pointing out how different his own philosophy is. This criticism is very shrewd and largely justified, yet somewhat unfair. Green fails to maintain a clear distinction between his theory of general human practice and his moral theory. In the same vein, he fails to acknowledge the extent to which his philosophy and utilitarianism overlap. The strength of his moral theory might have been more accessible if he had explored the elements in common with utilitarianism, rather than rejecting them.

Green claims that while for the utilitarians 'the good generically is the pleasant, in [his] treatise the common characteristic of the good is that it satisfies some desire'.[9] Expanding on this subtle distinction, Green claims: 'We cannot think of an object as good, *i.e.* such as will satisfy desire, without thinking of it as in consequence such as will yield pleasure; but its pleasantness depends on its goodness, not its goodness upon the pleasure it conveys.' It follows that 'desirable' and 'pleasurable' are not identical because the variety of human desires is greater than the scope of anticipated pleasures. The upshot is that we have desires for things that cannot be described as pleasant. This distinction is very important to Green since, to a considerable extent, it is the basis of his moral theory. However, he is also giving us reasons to believe that, apart from important differences, there are also important similarities between his and the utilitarian doctrines.

Basing the concept of the good either on what is pleasant or on what is desirable reveals, in equal measure, the understanding that the individual is the centre of human practice. Employing much less philosophically precise vocabulary than Green's, the utilitarians propound a very similar understanding of human practice. According to Green, 'what is common to all acts of willing' is that in them 'a self-conscious individual directs himself to the realisation of some idea, as to an object in which for the time he seeks self-satisfaction'.[10] The object of desire is the product of a self-projecting individual: in his desires 'a man is an object to himself'.[11] The self-conscious individual is the focal point of human practice as all objects of desire (and therefore all that is 'good') are related to a willing subject. This is the formal rule of human practice, as well as the general definition of what is good. 'Self-satisfaction is the form of every object willed.'[12] The utilitarians' claim is very similar. Green's understanding of the pursuit of self-satisfaction as a principle is the same as the utilitarians' understanding of pleasure. They thought that whatever the nature of one's particular action, the pursuit of happiness was at its root. It is true that 'self-satisfaction' is a more accurate term than 'pleasure', yet the difference in the meaning does not justify the huge gap Green would like to see between his and the utilitarian theory.

According to Green, utilitarianism fails to produce a satisfactory moral theory because it gives a false account of the generic nature of desire. Utilitarians claim that in every desired object a person seeks a state of her own pleasure. Green argues that this is wrong. The fact that the achievement of a particular aim brings me pleasure does not mean that my action was motivated by the anticipation of pleasure. It may be the case that I seek the pleasure itself, but it may also be the case that I do not aim at pleasure; rather, the pleasure comes as a consequence of what I have achieved.[13] Utilitarians are wrong to believe that people pursue pleasure. Green instead argues that human beings pursue 'self-satisfaction', and his purpose is 'to bring out more clearly the distinction between the quest for self-satisfaction which all moral activity is rightly held to be, and the quest for pleasure which the morally *good* activity is not'.[14]

This criticism of utilitarianism is unfair as it reveals Green's misconception of his own transcendental rule. The utilitarian claim that in his desires an agent seeks pleasure is very similar to what Green means in saying that in his desires an agent seeks self-satisfaction. Green's criticism of the utilitarian principle would apply with equal force to his own rule. What is important about Green's transcendental rule is its *formal* character. In every object of desire we *ultimately* seek satisfaction.[15] Even if our concrete action does not aim at immediate self-satisfaction – let us say, I give up my coffee break in order to finish a paper on time – this action is still motivated by a valued image of myself. In Book II Green makes it clear how the meaning of an action is determined by its relatedness to one's general well-being. According to Green's transcendental rule, the pursuit of self-satisfaction does not imply selfishness, but an ultimate unity of all the diversity of one's behaviour. The work of a self-distinguishing and self-seeking consciousness finds expression in the quest of an idea of self-satisfaction.

Green and the utilitarians have a very similar understanding of the general format of human practice: both parties believe that the individual is the 'centre' of human practice. Things acquire their meanings and value according to their relation to a desiring human being. We can see that both Green and the utilitarians adopt a phenomenological perspective in defining the nature of the good. The content of the good is seen to derive from the desires of the individual. Like Green, the utilitarians attempted to define morality from an inner personal perspective. The rejection of all substantive values and the recourse to pleasure express their intention to eliminate any dogmatic assumptions about 'the good'. As Timothy Sprigge puts it, the 'essential impulse behind utilitarianism is the sense that the only criterion of something really being intrinsically good is that it feels good'.[16] In their definition of what is good and what is morally good, they tried to be faithful to what every individual actually craves for. Their theory conveys in simpler terms Green's idea that the good is a projection of a self-objectifying consciousness.

By criticising utilitarianism Green wants to make a vital distinction to his moral theory: a distinction between pursuing things for the pleasure they bring us and pursuing things regardless of whether they will or will not bring pleasure. However, this distinction is also challenging to his own theory of human practice. The introduction of the concept of the 'moral good' as something that is valuable in itself challenges not only utilitarianism but also Green's transcendental rule.

The problem raised by the introduction of the concept of the 'moral good' is how it is possible to claim that something is valuable in itself. Whatever the object of our aspiration is, it is aspired to under the guise of self-satisfaction. Nothing is an absolute object of desire; each particular object becomes an object of desire only in its relation to one's scheme of values. Expressed in other words, the problem we are facing is the problem of the transition from the formal rule of general human practice to the formal rule of moral practice. In the opening section of Book III, Green states this very clearly:

> Granted that, according to our doctrine, in all willing a self-conscious subject seeks to satisfy itself – seeks that which for the time it presents to itself as its good – how can there be any such intrinsic difference between the objects willed as justifies the distinction which 'moral sense' seems to draw between good and bad action, between virtue and vice?[17]

This problem can be resolved, and we shall deal with it in more detail in the next section. When Green says that something is an aim in itself, he means that we pursue it for a reason other than the pleasure we will experience in obtaining it. He is right to believe so. However, doing something for itself, not for personal benefit, does not alter the general framework under which we act. This is the main point: the functioning of this framework does not imply in the least that all we do is only a means to an end. The formal rule does not mean that in all our aspirations we think of pleasure or self-satisfaction. The formal rule says nothing about the manner in which we pursue particular objects, and this is what is important from a moral point of view.

2.2 The difference between the pursuit of pleasure and the pursuit of the moral good

Had Green defined his criticism of the utilitarians more precisely, the advantages to his moral theory would have come across much more sharply. It is not true that people do not pursue pleasure because, as Green himself earlier argued, they act within the framework of self-satisfaction. We do not have grounds to believe – nor does Green give us any – that 'pleasure' and 'self-satisfaction' are two substantially different phenomena. The important point in Green's moral philosophy is the observation that within the general framework of pursuing self-satisfaction, a serious divergence exists between different types of actions depending on the motivation out of which they are performed. The change in motivation reflects a substantive change in the nature of the action. Defining the nature of moral action hinges on explaining the difference between the pursuit of immediate self-satisfaction and the pursuit of an object believed to be good because it does more than gratify the acting agent. The fact that an overarching framework of human conduct exists does not prevent the possibility of substantial differences of action within it.

As I have pointed out earlier, both Green and the utilitarians adopt a phenomenological perspective when defining the nature of the good. Staying with this terminology, one can say that Green's argument is that the utilitarian theory is phenomenologically incorrect or imprecise. This is because even if individuals act within the general framework of pursuing self-satisfaction, their various actions are guided by different types of motivation. It is important to observe that not all desires are accompanied by the thought of gaining pleasure. Green criticises the utilitarians from the same (phenomenological) perspective they are trying to adopt. His argument is that, from the perspective of one's personal experience, pleasure is not the only thing one cherishes. As individuals, we are capable of pursuing a motivation more complex than pleasure; we are capable of overcoming the drive for pleasure in view of a further goal. We can pursue objects which we believe to be good for reasons other than the attainment of personal gratification.

Green explains moral agency by describing the nature of our desire to achieve self-perfection. He points out that this desire has a different status from every general desire. It is a desire performed in a disinterested manner. As the state of perfection is always not yet attained, one never has an absolutely clear vision of its content. So it is not exactly the anticipation of pleasure, but rather the belief in the value of self-perfection which motivates one to pursue its attainment:

> ... because it is the fulfilment of himself, of that which he has in him to be, it will excite *an interest in him like no other interest, different in kind from any of his desires and aversions* except such as are derived from it. *It will be an interest as in an object conceived to be of unconditional value* ...[18]

We can see then that explaining the content of the moral ideal becomes an explanation of the ways in which we, as human beings, come to seek the attainment of this ideal. So morality consists in the 'moral' manner in which an object is pursued. That is why the formal definition of moral behaviour reflects the inner attitude out of which an agent pursues a particular object. For people who pursue the moral ideal, 'it will express itself in their imposition on themselves of rules requiring something to be done irrespectively of any inclination to do it, irrespectively of any desired end to which it is a means, *other than this end, which is desired because conceived as absolutely desirable.*'[19]

What characterises moral behaviour is that a person overcomes his spontaneous pursuit of pleasure. Although he continues to be generally determined by the transcendental rule, he looks for self-satisfaction in objects which he believes are good in themselves. In the general framework of acting in the pursuit for self-satisfaction, he nevertheless pursues an object in a self-disinterested manner. This definition of morality is phenomenological as it analyses the process in which one's general behaviour becomes moral by tracing the path of personal experience one goes through in this process.

Now we can address the paradox that something could be valuable in itself, which we discussed in the previous section. The point is that as all objects of our desire are objects in which we seek ourselves, there is not a single object that can be valuable in itself, in an absolute way, or as an end. All objects are part of the context of our general pursuit of self-satisfaction. However, these expressions still have meaning. To strive for something for its own sake means to strive for it in a self-disinterested manner. It means striving for it without thinking about the self-satisfaction we will derive, striving for it in spite of the fact that it may be good for us. So all claims that certain objects possess absolute value are, in fact, claims about the manner in which we pursue them. The assertion of intrinsic value is an assertion of an attitude. To believe in the intrinsic value of an object means that the person who so believes has overcome, with respect to this particular object, the self-centred pattern of her behaviour.

Taken alone, both the utilitarian theory and Green's theory of human practice leave us short of an explanation of moral behaviour. The explanation of morality needs an additional element to the formal rule of human practice: a moral agent pursues an object of self-satisfaction with a self-disinterested motivation. Seemingly, the two formal rules contradict each other. If moral behaviour implies overcoming our spontaneous pursuit for self-satisfaction, how can we claim that all human behaviour takes place within the format of self-satisfaction? Green's answer is that human beings have the capacity to act unselfishly; they can see their well-being as consisting of goods that are not purely personal but that hold intrinsic worth. The reconciliation between the two formal rules, which Green could have offered, is that in moral conduct we maintain the overarching framework of self-satisfaction, but our motivation changes.

2.3   The moral ideal as the perfection of man

So far I have discussed Green's formal definition of morality which outlines the necessary features of moral conduct. We have seen that explaining moral behaviour and the nature of the object of moral pursuit hinges on an understanding of moral desire. Moral desire is a particular type of desire – it is a desire for an object that is good in itself. As discussed in the previous section, an object is good in itself if it is pursued with a self-disinterested attitude. The moral character of the object of someone's pursuit is derived from the agent's moral disposition. The same object can be either moral or morally neutral depending on the attitude, or the type of desire, with which it has been pursued. Green argues that his doctrine, unlike the utilitarian one, defines the distinction between what is moral and what is not on the basis of 'motives' and not of the 'effects' of one's actions.[20] The formal definition of moral behaviour is such that it leaves the objects of moral pursuit open for specification. However, parallel to his formal definition, Green offers a substantive one.

Green points out that strict Benthamite utilitarianism fails to offer philosophical support for what is both a common-sense conviction and the view propounded by J. S. Mill, namely, that 'some kinds of pleasure are more desirable and more valuable than others'.[21] This view is unsustainable within the theoretical framework of utilitarianism. 'The strict Benthamites hold that such differences of kind between pleasures as arise from differences in their exciting causes only affect their value or the degree of their goodness, in so far as they affect the amount of pleasure enjoyed on the whole.'[22] So Mill's belief in 'the intrinsic superiority of the higher [pleasures]' is incompatible with the general spirit of the utilitarian doctrine to which he has committed himself.[23] Because, for the utilitarians, all value is rooted in the desire for pleasure, higher value can only be derived from a greater amount of pleasure. The utilitarian doctrine not only cannot account for Mill's belief in the important difference between higher and lower pleasures, but it also goes against our intuition. Green points out that if we are asked whether all desires have the same status, the answer would be negative. Some of our desires 'we think well of in ourselves', yet some we condemn.[24] Our belief that some objects of desire are better than others presupposes a concept of an object that is considered as best.

According to Green, the moral ideal is the 'best state of being for man – best in the sense that in it lies the full realisation of his capabilities, and that in it therefore alone he can satisfy himself'.[25] The moral ideal is 'the true good'. 'It is an end in which the effort of a moral agent can really find rest.'[26] Green is aware that his statement of the existence of a true good, of an ultimate object of desire, is a challenging one and it is likely to provoke a lot of disagreement. He anticipates accusations that he is 'making huge assumptions' by 'taking for granted that there is some best state of being for man'.[27] I would distinguish three main arguments which Green develops for the purpose of substantiating his theory. First, he claims that 'there is a consciousness for and in which [the fulfilled human spirit] really exists'.[28] Secondly, he argues that the existence of a perfect state of man's development is already implied in our concept of progress. Thirdly, Green claims that some institutions and habits testify to a particular direction of the development of the human character. I will review these in turn.

Non-believers may find Green's moral theory dubious because of the claim that the human state of perfection exists 'as already present to some divine consciousness'; that 'as our knowledge, so our moral activity was only explicable on supposition of a certain reproduction of itself, on the part of this eternal mind'.[29] If the concept of the moral ideal rests on the assumption of a divine consciousness that reproduces itself in human beings, then many contemporary readers may doubt the existence of such an ideal. A careful examination of this argument, however, will show that Green's vision of the divine consciousness virtually restates his theory of human practice. It reveals his understanding of how human practice is dependent on the way human consciousness works. To remind ourselves, Green argues that in his actions 'a self-conscious individual directs himself to the realisation of some idea, as to an object in which for the time he seeks self-satisfaction'.[30] Human practice is characterised by 'self-seeking' and a 'self-distinguishing principle', so that in all her actions an individual is an object to herself. In all her desires an individual pursues objects related to her well-being and, Green adds, related to her image of herself.

The function of the divine consciousness in Green's moral theory is to explain the origin of the idea of the true good/the moral ideal.

It is given to us by virtue of the process through which the eternal mind self-objectifies itself in human minds. However, this function becomes superfluous in view of the fact that Green provides another, much better explanation of the origin of the moral ideal. The concept of a better state of ourselves is generated in the course of human practice due to its self-objectifying character. In all his desires an individual pursues an idea of his well-being, an idea of something which he is not at the moment, but may become in future:

> It is thus that he not merely desires but seeks to satisfy himself in gaining the objects of his desire; presents to himself a certain possible state of himself, which in the gratification of the desire he seeks to reach; ... that he has the impulse to make himself what he has the possibility of becoming but actually is not ...[31]

I believe that Green's argument could have been stated more effectively in the following way. The fact that we try to improve ourselves in an effort to achieve self-perfection is implied in our capacity to pursue ever more complex concepts of what is good. By pursuing an ever more advanced concept of our well-being we end up developing our own character. Human practice is such that the quest for self-satisfaction results in self-development. We pursue perfection because we are capable of self-improvement. If asked why this is so, Green could have replied in exactly the same way as he replied to the question, how can he prove the existence of the divine mind? 'Proof of such a doctrine, in the ordinary sense of the word, from the nature of the case there cannot be. It is not a truth deducible from other established or conceded truths.'[32] The transcendental rule of human practice cannot be proved by deducing it from other truths – it serves as a basis of other arguments.

Green's second argument about the moral ideal is that it is implied in our concept of progress. If we believe in progress, this already means that we have some idea about a final purpose or an end. Green rejects the belief that human development can take the form of endless successive stages, none of which is more important than the others. 'If there is a progress in the history of men it must be towards an end consisting in a state of being which is not itself a series in time ...'[33] The ideas of progress and development imply an understanding of the positive movement towards something of greater worth, which in turns implies a vision of something of ultimate worth. This argument is tied to the previous one. We have a notion of progress, and accordingly a notion of ultimate worth, because we are self-conscious individuals who have 'the idea of an absolute value in a spirit which we ourselves are'.[34]

Green's third argument in support of the moral ideal is that the human pursuit of perfection is exemplified by 'the actual progressive realisation of human capacities in knowledge, in art, and in social life'.[35] The emergence of certain institutions and habits which facilitate the process of human fulfilment provides a practical testimony to the gradual progress of humankind towards the ever fuller implementation of the moral ideal. Later, in Chapter V of Book III of the *Prolegomena*, Green analyses how 'a higher moral standard is possible for the Christian citizen than was possible for the Greek of Aristotle's age', referring to the fact that the concept of the brotherhood of man was lacking in antiquity and was introduced by Christianity.[36]

Green refers to the 'moral ideal', the 'true good' and the 'unconditional good' as the same thing: this is the perfection of the human character. The fulfilled human spirit, for Green, holds unconditional value. Whether the perfect character necessarily represents a moral good, I believe, is an open question.

2.4 The phenomenological circle

Green shows that a moral philosopher necessarily argues circuitously, while trying to explain the nature of moral behaviour. On the one hand, he explains the moral ideal, or the unconditional good, by claiming that it is what the good will is directed towards. On the other hand, he explains the good will as the will for the unconditional good:

> If, on being asked for an account of the unconditional good, we answer either that it is the good will or that to which the good will is directed, we are naturally asked further, what then is the good will? And if in answer to this question we can only say that it is the will for the unconditional good, we are no less naturally charged with 'moving in a circle'.[37]

Green argues that this circle may be easy to disguise, but it is difficult to avoid. Kant, for example, seems to have focused his definition of morality entirely on 'good will'. However, Green argues that the German philosopher's definition implies, yet fails to spell out, the assumption of unconditional good.[38] Let me explain why this circle becomes inevitable.

The moral ideal is the perfection of man, but what this perfection consists in can never be known in advance 'because it consists in the realisation of capabilities which can only be known in their ultimate realisation'.[39] As quoted earlier, the moral ideal is an end in which the effort of the moral agent can find rest. So in a way, one can form 'some negative conclusion': 'that this realisation [of our capacities] can only be attained in certain directions of our activity, not in others'.[40] The definition of the moral ideal is essentially related to describing the constitution of the moral agent. A moral agent pursues an object in a self-disinterested manner; she does not desire it because of the pleasure it will bring to her, but because she believes this object carries worth higher than her own self-satisfaction. As discussed in section 2.1, it is her readiness to overcome her pursuit of immediate pleasure that characterises her as a moral agent. The quest for self-fulfilment qualifies as moral action because this quest is carried out with a moral disposition. The desire for self-fulfilment differs from any ordinary desire for pleasure – it is a form of overcoming the desire for pleasure. Green summarises the moral disposition for action by the term 'good will'. That is why he claims that the unconditional good, or the moral ideal, is that which is the object of the good will.

It seems that there should not be a problem. Green defines the moral good through the good will, and the good will as the disposition for self-disinterested action. Why does he claim that we need to define the good will as the will for the unconditional good? Green's critique of Kant and the utilitarians provides the answer.

Green is aware that his formal account of morality is very similar to Kant's. While he claims that morality is a voluntary 'imposition on [our]selves of rules requiring something to be done irrespectively of any inclination to do it', for Kant it is 'the will to conform to a universal law for its own sake or because it is conceived as a universal law'.[41] Such a formal definition seems to avoid the necessity of reference to the unconditional good, and therefore, to avoid 'the circle'. This, however, is so only on the surface. As mentioned earlier, Green points out that Kant's principle implies an unconditional good: 'the recognition of the authority of such a universal law must be founded on the conception of its relation to an unconditional good'.[42] In order to explain Green's concern and to bring out his point in clearer terms, I need to expand Green's argument. Because the formal definition of morality focuses on the moral agent (by describing her disposition for action), it deliberately leaves open the specification of the object of moral pursuit. However, a moral philosopher should not underestimate the role of this object. The good will is always directed towards an object which is not in itself that good will. A moral agent aspires to do something not for the purpose of being a moral agent (he exercises his good will not for its own sake), but because he believes it is important to do so. I help others because I want to help them, not because I want to see myself as a moral agent. If the latter is what I am doing, the morality of my conduct becomes questionable. The good will and the object of the good will are two separate entities. Although they are connected (although the object of the good will derives its moral character from the good will), they do not and should not coincide. That is why the good will and the object of good will are in a circular relationship. I call this a phenomenological circle as it represents a necessary feature of human practice: we are always directed towards something that is related to, but different from, us. This is another way of restating Green's transcendental rule.

Utilitarians, Green argues, appear to avoid 'the circular' problem in defining morality. If they claim that the unconditional good is pleasure, and the good will is that which effectively produces the greatest amount of pleasure, then they are not trapped in the difficulty of defining two new concepts by deriving each from the other. Green claims, however, that they fail to define morality altogether. His argument is that they take the 'good will to be relative to something external to itself; ... to an end wholly alien to, and different from, goodness itself'.[43] On account of their theory they cannot claim that the perfection of man and of society is an end in itself.

Again, a little further explanation will help to present more forcefully the point of Green's criticism.

The utilitarian theory fails to give philosophical sanction to the common intuition that some desires are better than others, that some things carry higher value than others irrespective of the amount of pleasure attached to them. Green's moral theory leads us to believe that the formal way of defining morality focuses on our capacity to overcome spontaneous desire for pleasure. In this sense, Green argues that pleasure is 'alien to, and different from, goodness itself'.[44] An important aspect of the moral good is that the agent has overcome her spontaneous pursuit of pleasure. Utilitarians avoid the complication of circular definitions, but at the cost of bypassing a difficulty that is necessary in explaining morality. The moral ideal exemplifies one's capacity to conceive of, and desire, something more than what is good for oneself only. It is neither pleasure nor displeasure. It is difficult to pin down because it represents one's attempt to extend the boundary of what has so far been achieved. In this sense its character is fluid. Yet we have intuitions about what is good and we follow these intuitions as guidelines for our moral behaviour. The difficulty comes from the fact that, by definition, the moral ideal should be left unspecified, yet we cannot have a moral act without an implied understanding of what is good. In our moral actions we pursue values that are always concrete.

To conclude: The formal definition of morality leaves the moral ideal essentially unspecified, yet every concrete moral action pursues a particular vision of the good as distinct from moral motivation (the good will). If we commit ourselves to one, we are disloyal to the other. If we accept the perfect character to be the moral ideal, then we overrule self-disinterestedness as an absolute requirement for moral action: one can pursue self-perfection without acting from a moral disposition. If we take the good will to be the basic criterion of moral action, then we commit ourselves to the view that any object whatsoever can be moral so long as it is sought from a moral disposition. So neither defining a moral attitude nor defining a moral ideal is in itself complete and self-sufficient for the purposes of explaining moral action. Yet, defining both leads to contradiction.

2.5   The change of perspective

The circularity in explaining morality can be legitimised through the observation that the two definitions result from shifting the perspective from which the definition is made. The formal definition of moral behaviour is given from the perspective of the philosopher who aims to define the generic nature of morality. The substantive definition is given by the moral agent herself. It answers the question about the kinds of things that are worth doing, that are good not only for her, but good in principle. So while the 'intrinsic goods' cannot be specified in general, they are always specified in particular moral actions.

The first perspective can be seen as the external, or 'objective', perspective which focuses on the subjective conditions of moral action. The second is internal. It comes from a subjective standpoint and aims to arrive at objective grounds; it tries to discover what this good is that is good not only for oneself, but is unconditionally good and therefore worth the moral effort of overcoming one's spontaneous pursuit for pleasure. However, because these are two different perspectives pursuing answers to two different questions, the definitions they reach are definitions of two different things. Green's moral theory provides us with two definitions of morality – a formal and a substantive one – and it is important to underline their difference.

Green believes that the circular definition is a complication and so he tries to 'overcome' it. He is not aware that he is formulating two different definitions as his aim is to explain one and the same thing: the nature of moral action. He believes he is defining the same phenomenon in many different ways and he attempts to merge diverse explanations into a single and unitary one. Claims such as 'the only true good is the good will' reveal a tendency to conflate the two elements of the phenomenological circle.[45] The true good should be, on Green's account, the object of the good will. Therefore, I argue, it cannot coincide with the good will. As commented earlier, the desire of a moral agent is directed towards achieving something believed to be good, not towards being a moral agent.

Green tends to shift between the two different perspectives without accounting for this shift. For example, he uses 'the perfect character' both to name the moral ideal (that is, give a substantive definition) and to explain moral dispositions (which constitutes the formal definition). On the one hand, the perfection of man is a good in itself, and as such is the object of moral desire. On the other hand, Green believes that this is what we want to achieve because the perfect character will provide us with the proper disposition for moral action. So Green uses the concept of human perfection for the dual purpose of stating the unconditional good, and for promoting the idea of acting with moral intentions. This indiscriminate usage has caused legitimate confusions. Colin Tyler points out that, if, according to Green, the true good is

> a state of character, then the question arises, is it a disposition to act or a form of activity? ... Certainly, only a man of perfect character can perform perfect actions, and performing good actions fosters a better character. Yet, this assertion does not resolve the question of whether or not Green believes that the true good is possessed by good men all the time or merely when they are exercising their characters in practice.[46]

Tyler's point is that even if the perfect character and good actions are related, they are none the less two different entities. Because Green makes two references to the 'perfect character' with respect to its role in moral action, he should have made that clear in order to avoid making the controversial claim that good men are always moral. The terminology of the phenomenological circle can pinpoint and resolve this problem. When 'the good character' is referred to in the sense of a 'moral disposition for action', we should refer to the 'good action' as something different from it – as something that derives from, but does not coincide with, the perfect character itself.

2.6   Between deontology and consequentialism

Green's straddling of two, difficult to reconcile positions is reflected in David Weinstein's article 'Between Kantianism and Consequentialism in T. H. Green's Moral Philosophy'. Weinstein asserts that Green's moral philosophy is situated between Kantian formalism and utilitarian consequentialism; between understanding morality as obedience to a self-imposed law and understanding it as an attempt to achieve particular goals. Weinstein argues that Green's moral theory offers a kind of synthesis which is closer to utilitarianism. He claims Green is a 'dispositional' consequentialist and his philosophy is 'a genuine good maximising theory' where the good is defined as 'moral self-realisation'.[47]

Avital Simhony disagrees with Weinstein's conclusion that Green's liberalism accords with the terms of 'indirect utilitarianism'.[48] She argues that 'Green's liberalism is constructed as a direct challenge to utilitarian liberalism' and, therefore, 'we have much to lose from consequentializing or ulititarianizing Green'.[49] She believes that, if Green's philosophy offers a synthesis, it is on the deontological side:

> [Green] defends a kind of deontological theory which is both good-promoting and consequence-sensitive but which 'does not interpret the right as maximising the good'. He shares with Kant the equal respect for persons (which utilitarianism does not). ... At the same time, however, he shares with utilitarianism the importance of promoting the good (which Kant fails to do).[50]

I have argued that Green explores the nature of morality from two perspectives which cannot be employed simultaneously. On the one hand, he defines moral behaviour by exploring the capacity of human self-consciousness to overcome its self-centred disposition. He outlines the formal conditions of moral action as the desire to seek self-satisfaction in objects which do not bring immediate pleasure. Such a formal definition, however, leaves the object of moral desire unspecified as a matter of principle. This can be seen as the Kantian perspective in Green's moral philosophy. On the other hand, Green defines the moral good as the perfect character and thus gives a substantive description of that good. Whether this can be seen as a utilitarian perspective is contestable. Yet it is a different perspective for defining morality. Simhony claims that:

> [The] refusal to join in a discourse of dichotomies underpins Green's entire philosophical approach and may be described as a relational approach. Essentially his relational approach seeks to go beyond dichotomies by simultaneously rejecting the one-sidedness of each side of an opposition and interrelating elements of both into a new perspective.[51]

I agree with Simhony that Green overcomes the one-sidedness of both these perspectives taken separately. The difficulty, however, is that a synthesis cannot be achieved. This is Green's concern in describing the circular format of defining morality. The circle can

either be avoided at the cost of failing to explain moral agency altogether, as the utilitarians do; or unsuccessfully disguised as is the
case with Kant.

2.7   Is it the individual or her perfection that is an end in itself?

The shift between different perspectives brings a further challenge
to Green's moral philosophy. He can be seen as vulnerable to the
following accusation. If Green maintains the unconditional value of
the perfection of human character, he cannot be arguing at the
same time that the 'ultimate standard of worth is an ideal of *personal*
worth'.[52] Either all people are ends in themselves – at whatever stage
of development of character they happen to be – or it is human perfection that is of ultimate value, and those who actively pursue it
hold a higher status than those who do not.

When Green explains why the moral ideal is man's perfection, he
goes through two stages: first, he argues for the absolute value of the
human individual, and secondly, that human perfection is the ultimate end of human development. Although Green will not separate
the value of the human individual from the value of individuals'
perfection, we can see that these are two distinguishable issues and
each of them receives its own treatment in his philosophy. I will
briefly address each of them in turn.

The pathos and inspiration of the section from the *Prolegomena*
entitled 'The Personal Character of the Moral Ideal'[53] compares
favourably with the 'On Individuality' chapter of Mill's *On Liberty*. It
could equally serve as a classic text in the history of liberalism. While
explaining the nature of 'the one divine mind that gradually reproduces itself in the human soul', Green expresses his belief that human
personality is the only place where the human spirit can develop.[54]
No entity of super-personal character, such as a nation, for example,
can supersede the value of the human individual. By 'personality'
Green means 'the quality in a subject of being consciously an object
to itself'.[55] He claims that our 'ultimate standard of worth is an ideal
of *personal* worth'; that all 'other values are relative to value for, of, or
in a person'; that to 'speak of any progress or improvement or development of a nation or society or mankind, except as relative to some
greater worth of persons, is to use words without meaning'[56] – and

this because the individual is the 'home' of the spirit. 'Since it is only through its existence as our self-consciousness that we know anything of spirit at all, to hold that a spirit can exist except as a self-conscious subject is self-contradictory.'[57] Nothing is more worthy or more valuable than the individual because the individual is the spring of spiritual life. We can speak of the value of 'history or development of mankind', of 'progress towards a perfect organisation of society', or of 'achievements of great nations at certain epochs of their history', only as 'relative to a value for, of, or in a person'.[58]

Further, Green argues that development is intrinsic to human spirituality. The notion of progress is 'an expression of the same principle of self-objectification without which, as we have seen, there could be no such things as facts for us, for our consciousness, at all'.[59] Here Green develops all the arguments that we have discussed in section 2.3, that the moral ideal is to be found in human perfection. The logic of Green's overall argument is as follows. Because nothing is more valuable than the human individual, and because the nature of personal spirituality is such that it implies permanent development, the ultimate value is the value of the individual's perfection. As I have already made clear, we have two arguments here, which Green wants to employ towards one conclusion.

Green believes that human perfection is the essence of the nature of the human individual in the sense that every person has the capacity to develop. That is why he will not speak of the value of the individual and the value of individual's perfection as two different things. However, addressing the value of the person and the value of a person's perfection as the same thing can lead to conclusions which Green would not wish to embrace. If the perfect character is an end in itself, then individuals who have not fulfilled their potential are not ends in themselves. As Thomas Hurka points out in his book *Perfectionism*, standing for perfection can go hand in hand with sacrificing the value of equality or liberty:

> … critics worry that perfectionism is hostile to the modern political values of *liberty* and *equality*. Because it thinks some lives are better than others, they argue, regardless of whether people want or would choose them, it favours state coercion to force people into excellence.[60]

Green's perfectionism is not achieved at the cost of sacrificing liberty, equality or the value of the individual in her actual state of imperfection. His passionate defence of the value of the individual against all abstract notions of collective happiness guards Green's philosophy from this standard attack on perfectionism. However, we have to bring out the implicit message of his moral theory in order to deal with the difficulty of how both the individual and the individual's perfection can be ends in themselves if they are different things. There are two observations I would like to make: first, to point out that the dichotomy between the value of personality and that of perfection results from shifting perspectives; and secondly, to bring forward what is implicit in Green's moral philosophy: the notion of negative morality.

The intrinsic value of personality and the intrinsic value of human perfection are moral goods of two different perspectives – the external and the internal. Judging the worthiness of others, that is, adopting an external viewpoint, and judging our own worthiness, by taking an internal viewpoint, yield two different results. We should think about other people as absolutely valuable as they are. That is, we should exert moral effort in treating them as ends in themselves, whatever the stage of their personal development. When thinking of ourselves, we are entitled to value our state of perfection higher than our actual state. We should invest moral effort in improving ourselves. Commitment to perfectionism does not jeopardise one's belief in equality and the value of each human being. As Hurka claims, perfectionism reflects 'acceptance of *self-regarding* duties'.[61] He argues, that among contemporary philosophers the dominant view is that 'morality concerns only views that affect other people'. A great strength of perfectionism is that it contests this view and promotes the idea that people have moral obligations towards themselves.[62] In other words, contemporary philosophy over-employs the external perspective and neglects the internal perspective, which aims to discover the individual's moral duties towards herself.

2.8   Moral vulnerability and negative morality

Green is rather the opposite case: if anything, he over-employs the perspective from which one decides to pursue self-perfection. He sees morality in positive terms – as a duty to improve oneself, to work hard, to exercise will, to overcome selfishness. However, Green's polemic about the absolute value of the human individual is very powerful and contains important implications. By spelling those out, we can arrive at a concept of negative morality and, therefore, a basis for a theory of human rights (see Chapter 5). To speak of the absolute value of the human individual is to present her as an end in herself, and therefore, as a recipient of moral effort. Claiming that the individual is a good in itself means that an agent should aspire towards other individuals' well-being irrespective of whether this brings her direct personal satisfaction. Thus Green speaks of the individual as a recipient of moral energy, that is, as someone in need of moral treatment. The idea that perfection is intrinsic to human nature throws light on the nature of the good. It aims to answer the question about what it is that we, as human beings, need. The answer is that, if our nature is such that we permanently undergo personal development, then we need to be developed, we need to fulfil our capacities, we need to be treated as equals: we are morally vulnerable. If we are not treated as ends in ourselves, or if we are prevented from developing our faculties, we suffer. So, in a sense, Green invokes a definition of negative morality. Although his principal effort is directed towards presenting an image of the individual as positively moral, his defence of human individuality, as well as his belief that spiritual development is a basic feature of human nature, suggests the concept of moral vulnerability and, hence, of negative morality.

A negative definition of moral nature focuses not on our moral potential but on our moral needs. It addresses the issue of human dissatisfaction accompanying the denial of moral treatment and the lack of self-fulfilment, as opposed to the feeling of moral satisfaction that accompanies the achievement of self-improvement. Spelling out that the exercise of high faculties is associated with an increased possibility of suffering and humiliation makes us – as Green's readers – realise that the extent to which moral life is interwoven into our practical life is greater than we realise. We are moral beings because we suffer when we are unacknowledged, offended, ostracised, underestimated, not respected, not loved.

These developments of Green's moral theory will find direct application in understanding his views on freedom and human rights, issues dealt with in Chapters 4 and 5, respectively. The concept of negative morality will offer an alternative justification of human rights – alternative to Green's claim that rights are based on social recognition. Negative morality is also related to the concept of negative freedom: a concept that remains undeveloped in Green's political philosophy.

2.9 Conclusion

Green's ethics is based on defining the nature of moral desire and establishing a distinction between the 'good' and the 'moral good'. Green faces and deals with the difficult question of how it is possible to differentiate between what is moral and what is not, providing that 'in all willing a self-conscious subject seeks to satisfy itself' (section 2.1). Expressed in other words, this is the difficulty of reconciling the formal rule of human practice (section 1.4) with the formal conditions of moral behaviour (section 2.2). Green partly disguises this difficulty by dissociating firmly his own philosophy from the utilitarian doctrine and thus, in effect, distancing his moral theory from his own theory of human practice. The advantages and insights of his ethics, however, come across much better when the common grounds are properly acknowledged at the outset. One important common ground is the phenomenological perspective in defining the nature of the good.

Green offers us two definitions of morality: a formal and a substantive one. I believe that both can be justified if the different perspectives from which they are asserted are clearly specified. These two definitions resolve two problems. The formal definition addresses the question: 'How can I be moral?', which is answered: by being good; by having good will; by willing to exercise my energies for a good purpose. The substantive definition addresses the problem: 'How do I know that what I believe to be good is actually good?' This problem expresses a desire to overcome one's personal vision of what is good and reach an 'objective' view.

These two definitions reflect the two elements of the phenomenological circle: the moral desire and its object (section 2.4). The formal definition of the moral ideal attempts to capture the attitude, the inner disposition through which moral behaviour is performed. The substantive definition aims to reflect the particular object in which moral action can be expressed. However, if these two definitions are given without any additional attempt of reconciliation, they contradict each other. As the substantive definition aims to pin down the *unconditional* good, this good is declared to be moral, irrespective of the nature of one's motivation. This contradicts the formal definition, according to which one's good will is *the condition* for the moral nature of any action. The indiscriminate shift between the two different perspectives leads also to contradicting statements about what is of ultimate worth: the human individual or the individual's perfection (section 2.7). I have argued that both, in turn, represent the answers to two different moral quests – the quest of treating others as ends in themselves, and the quest for self-improvement. Although I criticise Green for failing to dissociate the value of personality from the value of personal perfection, I argue that by addressing them as the same thing, he achieves a further purpose. He invokes the idea of moral vulnerability and, related to this, the idea of negative morality. This concept will play an important role in giving a full account of Green's theories of freedom and rights in Chapters 4 and 5.

I have argued that Green's theory is phenomenological because his formal definition of moral action reflects the personal attitude of the moral agent. Describing 'attitudes', 'intentions' and 'motives' of one's behaviour is a phenomenological thing to do. Green's moral theory is phenomenological in one other aspect. This is an aspect specific to Husserl's phenomenology. Husserl's phenomenological reduction displays the process of self-transcendence that is necessary for the acquisition of apodictic knowledge. In the Introduction (section 4) I argued that the same process of personal-reorientation can be seen as a central element of moral behaviour. The transition from the pursuit of the good to the pursuit of the moral good involves bracketing of the self-centred motivation on which human practice is generally based. Exploring the possibility of this inner transformation is an essential part of explaining moral behaviour. Green's moral philosophy is phenomenological because it develops the idea of suspending habitual personal attitudes – a process later described by Husserl in the phenomenological reduction.

3
Green's Theory of the Common Good[1]

The theory of the common good completes Green's moral theory. So far we have discussed the formal and the substantive descriptions of morality as presented in the first two chapters of Book III of the *Prolegomena*. The theory of the common good is developed in the third and fourth chapters of Book III and they will be the object of discussion in this chapter. We shall see that the full realisation of the individual's capacities is only one side of the moral ideal, the other being the pursuit of the well-being of others. In this sense the concept of the common good rounds up Green's moral theory. It gives further specification of both the formal and the substantive definitions of moral behaviour. As with his theory of morals, Green's common good theory contains two legitimate but distinguishable senses of the common good. In its first sense the common good should be understood as the principle of personal moral growth. In this sense it represents a theory laying down the formal conditions of moral action. It develops further the already given formal definition of morality as an activity performed in a self-disinterested way. The second sense is the common good as the society of equals. It expands the already given substantive definition of morality as the state of human perfection.

This observation contributes towards a better understanding and a reconstruction of Green's common good theory. So, on the one hand, it helps respond to the standard challenges of the kind 'Is there such a thing as a common good?', 'What is the common good?', 'Does the common good theory give a credible representation of human nature?' On the other hand, it develops new criticisms and offers reconstructions of his philosophy. Green does not spell out that the pursuit of the common good represents a process of moral growth. If the best spirit of his own common good theory is followed, we shall see that the common good does not reflect the innate moral nature of the human agency – as Green believes to be the case – but rather the innate *possibility* of moral behaviour.

The double usage of Green's common good has been registered in the critical literature.[2] What has not been done and is offered here is an analysis of the reasons why Green has ended with two definitions of the common good, an assessment of the dialectics between moral good and 'ordinary' good, and an inquiry into whether the common good represents a moral or an 'ordinary' good. The analysis of the first sense of the common good advances further the discussion about the formal conditions of the moral act started in the previous chapter. While the first definition of morality provided us with the formal rule of moral behaviour (section 2.2), the first sense of the common good reflects the process of transition from morally neutral to moral behaviour (sections 3.2 and 3.3). In the previous chapter I argued that general human practice on the one hand, and moral practice on the other, are guided by different formal rules. Green's common good theory explains the process of transition from the one to the other. The theme of the common good continues the phenomenological analysis of moral action and gives us grounds for the following conclusions. First, moral conduct can be undertaken only personally; secondly, the 'ordinary' good always remains a component of the moral good; thirdly, in its substantive use (its second sense) the common good is more likely to represent 'ordinary' good than moral good. This chapter introduces the concept of 'ordinary' good and investigates the dialectics between it and the moral good. Green equates the common good exclusively with the moral good and thus (i) 'loses' the concept of the ordinary good; (ii) fails to assess the dialectics between ordinary and moral good; and (iii) does not see that the meaning of the common good changes according to the perspective from which it is being defined.

As this chapter is very critical of Green, I would like to make clear at the outset that I have gained the philosophical grounds for my criticism by employing elements of Green's own moral and common good theories. My claim that the pursuit of the common good is a result of a process as opposed to being an intrinsic feature of the human character, as well as my analysis of the genealogy of moral behaviour, are based on the 'salvation argument' (section 3.3), which is the main component of Green's common good theory.

This chapter is structured as follows. Section 3.1 explains why Green has developed two concepts of the common good rather than one. A brief review of the previous chapter reminds us that Green has already developed two distinguishable definitions of the moral ideal in his moral theory which precedes the introduction of the common good. I argue that Green has followed the same strategy in the analysis of the common good by offering, first, a formal account, and second, a substantive account. Section 3.2 discusses the first sense of the common good. I argue that the primary purpose of Green's common good theory is to reveal the process through which an individual acquires the motivation to act as a moral agent. That is why the common good in the first sense reveals a process of personal growth. I argue that Green himself has not articulated straightforwardly the meaning of the common good as a process of personal development because he wants to present human morality as something that is fixed and unconditional, rather than dynamic (section 3.3). Further, I investigate the implications of the interpretation of the common good. Section 3.4 discusses the unique position of the self in the pursuit of the common good, and section 3.5 considers Green's loss of the concept of the ordinary good. Section 3.6 addresses the second sense of the common good and argues that in its substantive use the common good is not a moral good but an ordinary good.

3.1   Outlining the two perspectives in defining the common good

Before starting his discussion of the common good, Green has already laid the foundations of his moral theory by making substantive philosophical claims. He has defined moral behaviour from two perspectives and has recognised that this constitutes a problem as it gives his overall theory a circular character. In Chapter 2, I argued that his circular reasoning was not a drawback but a necessity; I therefore called it a 'phenomenological circle'. The phenomenological circle reflects the fact that whatever way of defining a moral good a philosopher adopts, he should be aware that this is one of two possible ways, neither of which is complete in itself or independent of the other. Green has defined the moral ideal in two ways. The first definition is given from the perspective of describing one's inner attitude, that is, by explaining the inner moral disposition. The actual objects in which this disposition can be practically enacted can vary and that is why they are left unspecified. For this reason I call this first definition of the moral ideal a 'formal' definition.

Green also defines the moral ideal from the perspective of specifying the actual object in which the moral good is to be found. As a moral philosopher, Green felt that he had to be able to give a direct answer to the question: 'What is the moral good?' He knew that his theory could be seen as inferior to the utilitarian one, which clearly and unambiguously named 'the greatest sum of pleasures' as the true good. That is why Green also gave a name to the moral good by claiming that the only true good is the perfect character. Thus Green believed that he escaped 'the circle'. It seemed that 'the perfect character' defined the moral ideal from the two perspectives simultaneously. It could represent both the disposition for moral action (people of perfect character always act with good will) and the object of the moral action (the perfect character seen as the achievement of a moral effort). My criticism of Green is that he should not have tried to 'overcome' the phenomenological circle. Defining morality from two perspectives has been a philosophical achievement. Green's attempt to avoid a circular definition of the moral good has left him unaware that his theory has offered two definitions of the moral ideal, rather than one.

As was the case with the moral ideal, Green defines the common good from two perspectives. Again, he felt uncomfortable with each of them separately, and that is why he tried to unify them in a single, straightforward theory. Andrew Vincent also points out that Green has given us two definitions, both with respect to the true good and to the common good: 'On the one hand, the true or common good can be seen as a permanent interest which is non-competitive, namely a formal will to be good. On the other hand the true good can be explicitly identified with the realisation of individual capacities.'[3] Vincent believes that this duality is the 'central problem in Green's idea of the true good which also permeates his discussion of the common good'.[4] Geoffrey Thomas speaks about 'a logically harmless but expositionally awkward ambiguity in Green's use of "common good"'.[5] The first use of the common good adds another aspect of the definition of the true good – 'compossibility'. The second use refers to 'a network of social roles'. Thomas believes that the ambiguity arising from these different uses 'creates no confusion in Green's argument'.[6] I argue that this ambiguity is itself a result of confusion. It is a consequence of Green's tendency to shift between a formal and a substantive definition; in other words, it is a result of his failing to keep in focus the phenomenological circle while analysing moral phenomena. I will review the two definitions of the common good in turn.

3.2 The common good as personal moral growth

Green introduces his theory of the common good by claiming that an individual's idea of her own perfection is not an idea of 'an abstract or an empty self'.[7] Her vision of her perfect self is influenced by her interest in others. Her idea of her own satisfaction includes the satisfaction of others as well. 'The man cannot contemplate himself as in a better state, or on the way to the best, without contemplating others, not merely as a means to that better state, but as sharing it with him.'[8] The argument is as follows. Because one's 'idea of the absolutely desirable ... arises out of ... man's consciousness of himself as end to himself', and because the individual's concept of himself includes his relations to his fellow human beings, his idea of his best state incorporates in itself the well-being of the others too.[9] A person cannot contemplate her happiness as separated from that of those around her. So when she thinks of her own fulfilment, she by necessity associates this fulfilment with that of others. I pursue the common good when I act upon a presentation of the good of others as being my good.

We can see that the theory of the common good reflects the personal attitude through which one starts to think of one's well-being as inseparable from the well-being of others. This is the first and the more basic sense of the common good. It should be understood along the lines of the formal, the non-substantive, definition of moral behaviour. It outlines the conditions of moral conduct without specifying the actual moral deed itself. The formal conditions of a moral act are to be found in the personal disposition of the agent. In this sense, the common good is a state of mind, an attitude, a personal insight into the content of the true good. Understood in this way, the common good is not located in any particular object; it should not be understood as something that is good for all. Therefore the sceptical claim that people will never agree on what the common good is becomes irrelevant: the common good is not a specific object; it is a principle of moral action. The theme of the common good is a continuation of the discussion of what constitutes moral conduct, of what is, in more concrete terms, my inner state while I am pursuing my ideal for perfection. Green advances us towards the idea that our state of perfection consists in an attitude of perceiving our good as united to that of others.

Green's theory of the common good describes, in essence, a person's transition from pursuing ordinary good towards pursuing moral good. While an agent pursues the moral good with a self-disinterested disposition (section 2.2), no such requirement exists in the case of the pursuit of the ordinary good. Ordinary goods are all those goods that are morally neutral. The difference between these two is marked by a change in the agent's disposition. Moving from the pursuit of ordinary good to the pursuit of moral good involves a process of overcoming one's disposition to self-centredness. The theory of the common good reflects people's capacity to develop their ideas of the good. The object in which they seek self-satisfaction can be something that predominantly satisfies themselves. However, it may also be something that satisfies them and the others in equal measure. The reason why it is not immediately obvious that Green's common good refers to a process of moral growth is that he has been reluctant to acknowledge the dynamics of moral conduct. Green views moral nature as fixed, as firmly embedded in the human personality. He wants to present the aspiration towards the common good as a trait of human character. He claims that all people have a genuine interest in the well-being of others – what I would call a 'noble social interest'.[10] The noble social interest implies that the individual takes an interest in her fellow human beings for their own sake, that is, regardless of whether this brings her any personal benefits. There is, however, an ambiguity about whether this interest is a quality that individuals cultivate, or a quality that they necessarily possess on the grounds of their human nature. The shortcomings in maintaining the latter and the advantages of advancing the former will become clear later.

Green's desire to assert the 'factuality' of the noble social interest – the interest in other people as ends in themselves – leads him to undervalue the process of personal development implied in the notion of the common good. He would rather refer to a prehistoric development which was completed with the emergence of rational man. However, Green's theory contains a description of a process in which a person has started to perceive other people's good to be as valuable as his own. Green advances the argument that *in his desire to overcome his transient nature, every human being tends to invest his energy into social projects*. I will present this argument in more detail. For the purpose of convenience, I call it 'the salvation argument'. I demonstrate that this argument expresses Green's ambivalent attitude towards the fact that noble social interest emerges over time, that is, that it is an outcome of a process.

3.3   The salvation argument: criticisms and defence

Green's desire to present the individual's devotion to the good of others as an inherent aspect of human nature, contradicts his theory of the moral ideal as the effort for self-perfection, as 'a life of becoming, of constant transition from possibility to realisation, and from this again to a new possibility ...'[11] Green's intuition about the developmental nature of human personality pervades his entire philosophy. It is also present in the salvation argument.

Green's salvation argument is as follows. We, as human beings, may sometimes pursue pleasure, but we never think of our ultimate good in terms of pleasure. Utilitarians are wrong to believe that the individual imagines his happiness as a 'sum of pleasures'.[12] Pleasures are not incremental. A repetition of the same pleasure does not necessarily increase the feeling of being pleased. Pleasures are transient and after they have passed they leave a feeling of dissatisfaction. So when one thinks of an ultimate good, one does not imagine a maximum number of pleasures, but something radically different. One looks for an object which is permanently good, for an 'abiding satisfaction'.[13] Thus a person seeks his ultimate good in 'ideal objects, with which on the one hand he identifies himself, and which on the other hand he cannot think of as bounded by his earthly life, – objects in which he thinks of himself as still living when dead'.[14] An example of such an object is the well-being of one's family. A man has an 'interest in permanent good' and with it, an interest in his own permanency. He sees his permanent good in providing for the well-being of his 'kindred', and his permanency in the fact that his kindred will outlive him: 'Projecting himself into the future as a permanent subject of possible well-being or ill-being – and he must so project himself in seeking for a permanent good – he associates his kindred with himself.'[15] The emergence of the family Green believes dates as far back as human interest in the permanent good.[16] The institution of the family presupposes a person's ability to think of others as of herself.

Further, Green argues that the same link that exists between the individual and her kindred exists between the individual and society in general. This special type of link expresses Green's understanding of the individual's social nature. Society gives the individual an opportunity for immortality:

> At a stage of intellectual development when any theories of immortality would be unmeaning to them, men have already, in the thought of a society of which the life is their own life but which survives them, a medium in which they carry themselves forward beyond the limits of animal existence.[17]

The common good is the person's chance to transcend the 'perishing nature of pleasures' and the finite nature of her individual self.[18] The idea of the salvation argument is that a person can find her permanent good only when she starts to see her own good as united with that of others.

Green claims that there can be no contradiction between one's true good and one's dedication to the good of others, as these two, by definition, are identical. There may exist a tension between what constitutes my pleasure and someone else's pleasure. But because *my true good* is the object in which my permanent satisfaction is sought, it is something different from pleasure. It is good for me, on account of being good for others, on account of my desire to associate myself with them. The possible contradiction between me and the rest can occur within the quest for pleasure, but never in the quest for the true good: 'the distinction of good for self and good for others has never entered into that idea of a true good on which moral judgements are founded.'[19] Green's thought is not 'the good of all has to be good for me as well'. It is, 'my true good is possible only as a contribution to, only in alliance with, the good of the others.' Green's 'common good' is the individual's 'true good'. Separated from society a person has no permanent well-being.

The conclusion of the salvation argument is that every human being can achieve true fulfilment only through his integration within society. It asserts something as a matter of fact, rather than as a possibility. Several serious objections can be raised against it, and I will consider two. The first is that if one's true good as a disinterested service to others is simply a matter of course, then one deserves no moral approbation for performing it. Alan Milne points out that presenting the true good as non-contradictory to one's inclinations 'obscures the real sacrifice of personal self-interest which meeting moral demands may involve'.[20] He adds that this account of human nature leaves no place for the possibility of 'immorality as distinct from moral error'.

The second objection focuses more sharply on the dogmatic form of this argument. Presenting moral conduct as if it were a mere fact serves badly Green's intentions to bring forward the complexity of moral life. His argument is vulnerable to all claims bringing evidence which contradicts Green's belief that in his urge to overcome his finiteness, an individual seeks to integrate himself with society; that '[h]is own well-being [he] thus necessarily presents to himself as a social well-being'.[21] There are several plausible assertions which can be made to challenge Green's claim. The following three are examples: 'there are people who understand the transient nature of human life and are prepared to accept it' (people without moral ambitions); 'there are people who grow to be more and more self-indulgent and who dedicate their lives to the pursuit of pleasure as a matter of principle' (people with immoral ambitions); 'there are people who need to break through their liaisons with the social environment in order to find their true self-identity' (people whose moral conduct does not take the form of service to society). Each of these claims poses a threat to Green's argument by denying its universality. It is difficult – I would say, impossible – to assert complex phenomena as universal facts, as Green does. To argue that the phenomenon of human beings seeking their salvation through a process of social integration is a fact of human nature is a poor way of presenting a valuable insight. The truth of this observation should not depend on its applicability to every single human life.

Green's argument, however, contains a universal message. It explains why and how human beings are capable of acting as moral agents. The salvation argument is a practical application of the abstract philosophical assertion developed earlier in *Prolegomena* that in all his action an agent follows an idea[22] (section 1.4). There Green argues that human beings do not act upon instincts but always follow an idea of self-satisfaction; that they always 'distinguish' themselves from their desires; that even when they succumb to easy pleasures they are always aware of the costs of their choice. The salvation argument gives flesh to, and thus reveals the strength of, the theory of the will. According to the salvation argument, when individuals want to increase their well-being they pursue some form of lasting self-satisfaction, which is not found in any 'sum of pleasures'. What Green demonstrates through this argument is that human beings' idea of self-satisfaction is constantly evolving (section 2.3). Initially, one's idea of well-being can coincide with simple pleasures, but this idea will, by necessity, develop towards a radically different object. Because simple pleasures are transient and their passing leaves a sense of dissatisfaction they will gradually 'disqualify' as an idea of what is good for oneself. The quest for permanent self-satisfaction can be achieved only in some kind of good which transcends ordinary pleasure. Only by seeing the good in a new light, that is, only by changing her concept of her well-being, can a person find lasting happiness. Moral behaviour is possible because human beings are capable of pursuing an idea of a good which is not only good for themselves, but a good that is common between them and others. So the salvation argument reveals the principle of moral action. It explains the genealogy of moral motivation and thus the possibility of moral conduct.

Both the salvation argument and the principle of moral action reflect a process. Green reveals the logical steps of the process in which one adopts the common good as one's own good: people are aware that pleasures are transient; they need permanent satisfaction; they look for objects where lasting well-being can be found; they find these objects in the unification of their well-being with that of others. All these logical stages are actually stages of human experience, each of them building on the preceding one. So, in a sense, Green's argument is not dogmatic at all – it does not *presuppose* the noble social interest, it demonstrates it by disclosing its genesis.[23]

The backbone of the salvation argument consists in describing the process by which an individual comes to think of others as himself. This process is difficult to explain because it is 'counter-factual'. Obvious facts are that individuals distinguish themselves from others and act in their own interests. Cases of disinterested service to others are exceptional. Yet to prove the possibility of the common good as disinterested service to others, Green does not have to reject obvious facts. Once he has described the process through which one's concept of self grows to incorporate others within itself, it becomes obvious how self-interest can simultaneously be interest in the good of others. The strength of Green's argument is that he describes the human character as dynamic, rather than as fixed; the weakness is that he wants to assert moral attitudes as facts. Thus, although he makes important discoveries about human nature, he ends up with a distorted picture. Green asserts the 'factuality' of people being loving, caring and noble, at the expense of denying the 'factuality' of them being self-centred and antagonistic to others. He does not need to deny the latter in order to assert the former. On the contrary, humans become noble and good to others in their attempt to overcome their selfish impulses. A full account of the generic nature of morals requires admission of the fact that individuals pursue pleasures and prioritise their own well-being over that of others.

Admitting the dichotomy between personal pleasures and the concern for the well-being of others does not pose such a threat to Green's common good theory as many critics believe.[24] His mistake is confined to the fact of not registering that this difference exists at least at some level. Simhony argues, in defence of Green, that all those who believe that there is a tension between egoism and benevolence presuppose a 'dualist moral framework' which precludes the possibility of 'non-contingent connection between the two personal and moral concerns'.[25] I believe that Green's common good theory should not be defended by denying the conflict between the personal and the common good, but by emphasising the fact that his theory discloses a process of moral growth. The pursuit of his common good is not a fact; it is a moral achievement.

It reflects a process whereby the moral agent has overcome his habitual pursuit of simple self-satisfaction. In other words, the synthesis between my good and the common good is not given, but achieved. Green is very good at explaining the process by which a person's concept of her own good grows to embrace the good of others, but he fails to see the implications of this theory. The synthesis in the end does not preclude the dichotomy at the beginning; the former is based on overcoming the latter.

3.4   The unique position of the self

An important implication of the observation that the primary purpose of the common good theory is to reflect a process of moral growth is the recognition of *the unique position of the self* in the process of finding the common good. Because Green does not make sufficiently clear that the common good, in essence, represents a principle of moral action, he also does not see the necessity of distinguishing between what is *my* ultimate good and what is the good I can do for *others*. As a matter of principle, these two cannot be the same.

This argument is very similar to what is known as the 'asymmetry argument'. Thomas Hurka points out that the asymmetry argument is reflected in both Aristotle's and Kant's versions of perfectionism:

> In Aristotelian perfectionism ... there is an *asymmetry* in agents' abilities to bring about the good, one that makes them less able to promote others' perfection than their own. In favourable conditions they can produce their own excellence directly, but they have less power over others.[26]

In the *Metaphysics of Morals* Kant argues:

> It is contradictory to say that I make another person's perfection my end and consider myself obligated to promote this. For the perfection of another man as a person, consists precisely in his *own* power to adopt his end in accordance with his own conception of duty, and it is self-contradictory to demand that I do (make it my own duty) what only the other person can do.[27]

The asymmetry argument is understood to lead to the conclusion that nothing can be done to assist someone in his pursuit for self-perfection and, therefore, governments are not in a position to help citizens in their attempt to act as moral agents.[28] These conclusions, however, do not follow from the asymmetry argument: its point is that an agent can directly achieve only his own perfection, and can perform a moral conduct only on his behalf. This does not imply in the least that assisting someone to attain the necessary disposition for moral action is impossible.

Green maintains that a person should not distinguish between his own true good and that of others. Once we are aware 'what it is that we desire in desiring our own true or permanent well-being, it would seem that we have already answered the question, what it is that we desire in desiring the well-being of others'.[29] Once we have established that permanent well-being cannot be found in pleasure or in any sum of pleasures, then we should know that it is not pleasure that we have to provide for others in our desire to do them good. It has already been ascertained that the individual attains his true well-being by conceiving of his good as common between him and others. It is the same kind of well-being, Green believes, he should aim to achieve for others.

There is one sense in which what Green says is correct. An individual should not judge the good of others by a criterion different from that by which she judges her own. She should not think of the well-being of her fellow human beings in terms inferior to her own. However, Green is wrong in advancing the view that she should act towards other people's permanent good in the same manner as she acts towards her own. This is impossible in terms of the definition of what the true good is. If I find a permanent satisfaction in caring for others, I can act upon my belief. Yet if, for instance, my brother finds his true good in caring for others, I cannot achieve this for him. As the true good acts upon the individual's moral ideal, it is non-transferable. As 'the only true good is the good will',[30] the true good exists only as performed.

We are again facing the phenomenological circle. Keeping a clear vision of the dichotomy between good will and the actual good done is very important. Whatever contents of the good are asserted, it can only be legitimised as moral from the perspective of the manner in which it is pursued. A generous deed is also a moral deed only if it is performed out of a moral disposition. Nothing is truly good on its own: its moral character is always invested in it by an individual who searches for a permanent satisfaction by identifying himself with others. The contents of the actual true good cannot be separated from one's motives for seeking it and then declared as a standard object of moral pursuit. If Green's idea of true good is properly understood, it becomes clear that my true good can never be your true good. What is truly good for me *may* be truly good for you, but the very object in which I seek my true good cannot be the same as yours. You cannot exercise my higher faculties, nor can you do good to others on my behalf. The true good cannot be given or taken.

This problem has often been disputed among the critics of Green's work. What does he mean by 'good' – the objects aimed at, or the way in which an object brings gratification? H. A. Prichard argues that it is the latter.[31] He believes that on Green's initial definition of good as something that satisfies desire, the consistent use of the term should signify a 'feeling of satisfaction and gratification' and not 'the *realisation* of the thing desired'.[32] As he observes that a feeling of satisfaction and gratification can be excited only by a state of our own activity, he concludes that 'there cannot be such a thing as a good common to two different persons, unless the two so-called different persons are really one and the same, and so not different persons.' If Green is consistent in his presentation of the 'good', he should not use it in the sense of an object, but in the sense of a subjective feeling.

Peter Nicholson marks the dichotomy in Green's usage of the term 'good' as a 'substantive' and 'adjectival' use.[33] He argues against Prichard that it is not true that Green means the good in an adjectival rather than a substantive sense. Nicholson believes that Green's more important definition of the good is as an object, not as a source of satisfaction.[34] He reveals the internal connection between the two approaches in defining the good. Nicholson argues that the adjectival use is only a means to a further and richer definition of a substantive concept. As Green's concept of good develops into a concept of moral good, Green has legitimately moved from one substantive use to another. It is for the purposes of this transition that Green analyses the good as a source of satisfaction: 'Green has moved from a substantive to an adjectival use of "good", and this enables him to reach a new substantive use.'[35]

Nicholson believes that as the good should be understood as an object, not as a source of satisfaction, Prichard's argument fails. I believe the good should be seen as both these things and, therefore, Prichard is partly wrong, partly right. He is wrong to argue that the common good can never be common. The object in which the agent, who seeks the common good, finds satisfaction, is good for her in common with others. When I say that Prichard is partly right as he claims the common good is a 'feeling of satisfaction', I should also make clear that I disagree with the conclusions he draws from that. Prichard believes that thus defined, the common good is a subjective feeling and therefore something without universal validity. The observation that when the common good is used in its meaning of 'involvement in moral conduct' it is not common but private, does not undermine in the least the common good theory. This observation leads to the conclusion that the common good stands in a different relation to its agent and those who benefit from it. To the first, it is the true good; to the second, it is an ordinary good.

The common good, seen as the true good, can only be mine, never ours. It is common as between me and others, but not common as belonging to each of us in an equal way. I can aim at a good which is common – being a good teacher, for example – because in attaining it, many people benefit. My good is also good for my pupils. Yet, this good stays in a different relation to me and to my students. It is my, but not their, true good. This 'common good' is not their true good, because in attaining it they have not yet become involved in activity contributing to the well-being of others. We can see that, by definition, the true good as common good implies that the object in which satisfaction is sought satisfies not only the subject of the action but a wider circle of people.

Green's theory of the common good is a further explanation of his views on the moral ideal. In the same manner as the moral ideal, the common good is not necessarily fixed in any particular object. The common good can express itself in pursuit of different objects. '[K]eeping a family comfortably alive, without reference to the well-being of any wider society' is an expression of the common good in the same way as the 'composition of a book on an abstruse subject', or organising the 'sanitation of a town'.[36] The particular objects in which the common good is sought 'vary in different ages and with different persons, according to circumstances and idiosyncrasy'.[37]

What unifies all quests for the common good is a principle. It always reveals an interest in an object which is good both for the individual and her fellow human beings. In other words, the common good is always to be found in an object which can be desired only if the individual identifies himself with a wider range of human beings. In clarification of this principle, Green argues that this object in which the common good is to be found is not part of one's experience: it is an anticipation, it is an image projected into the future. As was the case with the moral ideal, it acquires its particular meaning throughout the process of its pursuit:

> The idea of the good, according to this view, is an idea, if the expression may be allowed, *which gradually creates its own filling.* It is not an idea like that of any pleasure, which a man retains from an experience that he has had and would like to have again. It is an idea to which nothing that has happened to us or that we can find in existence corresponds, but which sets us upon causing certain things to happen, upon bringing certain things into existence.[38]

We can see that an important part of the definition of the common good is its 'open-endedness', its conditionality on the manner of its quest. It comes into existence only as 'crowning with success' someone's effort towards it. Green's claim is that the common good is not part of our experience, it is always a projection into the future as 'it rest[s] not on instinct but on self-consciousness – on a man's projection of himself in thought into a future, as a subject of a possibly permanent satisfaction'.[39] One conclusion of this claim is that whenever the common good is a 'fact', whenever it has already happened, and is thus part of experience, it should always be seen as an achievement. The unity of my well-being with that of others, and respectively, my identity with a wider social environment, is never a 'mere fact', it is an attainment. It is an achievement of a self-conscious subject.

With respect to the common good – the common good seen as one's true good or as a moral ideal – its agent is always in a unique position. The synthesis between one's welfare and that of others, between oneself and society – the synthesis which is the core of the common good – is always achieved, never pre-given. Through the identity with society the agent achieves something which he did not have before, and he becomes something which previously he was not. It is true that the common good attained in the end is meant to be, and is, good in common to the agent with others. Organising the sanitation of a town makes the life of everyone – of the agent and of her fellow residents – more comfortable. However, this is good to the agent in one more sense, additional to that of increasing comfort. It is good for her as it is also her self-fulfilment. The common good is good for all, but it stays in a different relationship to its performer and its beneficiaries.

Green is wrong to argue that a person can work for other people's true good in the same way as he works for his own. He says that the individual can contribute to the true good of others by 'the realisation for them of the same objects' in which he finds his own happiness.[40] I have shown, by referring to Green's theory of the common good as a moral ideal, that it is impossible to realise the true good on behalf of someone else.

3.5   The loss of the concept of the ordinary good

Observing this particular inconsistency in Green's theory – the impossibility of the common good as a moral ideal to be common to all equally – can bring forward other conclusions. In the assertion of the true good Green 'loses' his concept of the ordinary good. This loss is caused not by a lack of insight into human nature – Green himself had introduced a perfectly acceptable concept of good – but by his unjustified eagerness to reject entirely the hedonistic utilitarian theory of pleasure. With the progress of his theory of the moral ideal Green rejects a notion which initially served as a foundation: the notion of the ordinary good. In the process of elucidating the nature of the true good, Green effectively disqualifies the ordinary good from being good at all. This devaluation of the ordinary good is related to his neglect of the importance of the self-centred framework of general human practice. If these two are neglected, the theory of the common good/true good/moral good loses its foundation. Additionally, their practical fulfilment becomes impossible. To repeat: by ordinary good I mean the good which is good to oneself only (not necessarily to the exclusion of others, but not necessarily to their inclusion), as opposed to the moral good, which is intended by its agent as a good common between him and others.

There is a benign paradox implicit in Green's theory of the noble social interest. It is the same kind of paradox that was discussed in Chapter 2 (section 2.2) – about the possibility of an object being good in itself. How can something be valuable in itself, if the value of this thing derives from the fact that it satisfies a person's desire? The paradox of the noble social interest is based on the same principle. How is it possible for an agent to care about others as much as he cares about himself, if in all his behaviour an individual is an end to himself? Revealing and resolving this paradox offers a key to resolving the difference between ordinary and moral behaviour. Green says that it is characteristic of the noble social interest 'that, to the man who is the subject of it, those who are its objects are ends, in the same sense in which he is an end to himself'.[41] This popular appeal to which Green subscribes – the appeal to love 'thy neighbour as thyself' – would, I argue, be meaningless if there were not something special in the way one treats oneself. The paradox is the following. How can I treat others as I treat myself, if what generally characterises my behaviour is that I am an end to myself?

What is so special about the individual's treatment of himself? What defines one's self-perception is the unconditional value of an individual to herself. Everything she does bears directly or indirectly on her own self. This represents an essential part of Green's theory of the will where he claims that human practice is based on a 'self-seeking' principle.[42] The individual is always the final end of her actions. A person does not have to justify to himself repeatedly the fact that everything he does is aimed at increasing his well-being: his well-being is of unconditional value to him. This is the meaning of the concept of an end. 'The end' is what marks the upper limit of an ascending line of important things. 'The end' is the absolutely valuable in relation to which other things acquire their significance. That is why speaking about plurality of ends always entails contradiction. If the end is the ultimate purpose, or the absolutely valuable, how can this be multiple?

Now we have spelled out the implications of a person's self-perception as an end to himself, we can see that the appeal to treat others as ourselves is a controversial one. This paradox can be resolved, but I believe it should first be admitted. It is possible to treat others as ends, but this will entail a change in one's self-perception. When I treat someone else as an end, that means that my self-awareness as an absolute end has been challenged. The self-centred framework of my action has been questioned, and as a result, weakened. It is a powerful message of Green's moral philosophy that human beings as rational agents can distance themselves from themselves and overcome their habitual attitudes. The individual has 'this power of contemplating himself as possibly coming to be that which he is not', he has the power to 'bracket' his self-perception as absolutely valuable.[43]

What Green sometimes ignores is that even when overcome, the self-centred framework is not invalidated. As we have seen, it is this framework that underpins one's concept of an end. It is because we are ends to ourselves that we understand that other people are also ends to themselves. The possibility of bracketing my absolute value and pursuing goods solely on account of them being goods for others does not mean that I stop pursuing goods that are goods only to myself. I will develop this further. The elimination of the self-centred framework would simultaneously imply a destruction of the possibility of doing good to others. In other words, by disqualifying the ordinary good, one also makes the common good impossible. I can pursue the common good only if others need ordinary goods. This is because to the recipients of my production of the good, the good I produce is ordinary. It is meant to satisfy them not as part of a wider community, but as ends to themselves. For me, my production of good to others is the true or the common good, because it is meant to satisfy me not as a sole subject, but as a subject who has identified herself with others.

Green understands the common good as a moral good which supervenes on the ordinary good. A person's concept of what is good progresses in such a way that the early stage of seeing his good as simply good to himself is surpassed by a later stage where he sees his good in conjunction with the good of others. His concept of his common good overrules his concept of his ordinary good. One's true good is more important to oneself than one's ordinary good. For the person who pursues the common good (the true good), his ordinary good has been overcome and, therefore, suspended. I go along with Green here, on the provision that this suspension is within the framework of a particular moral conduct. However, other people's ordinary good is not suspended. Furthermore, to the person who pursues the common good, other people's ordinary good becomes as important as her own. Their ordinary good becomes more important to her than it did before her engagement with the common good. So although on one level the ordinary good is suspended, on another it continues to exist. Green does not point out that the suspension of the ordinary good is, first, temporary as limited to the situation of moral action, and secondly, refers only to the moral agent and not to those to whom the moral act is directed.

These considerations can lead us towards a conclusion that is directly relevant to the second sense of the common good: the common good understood as an actual object that is good in common to all of us. The conclusion is that a good which is common to a number of people and stays in equal relation to all of them cannot be a common good in the sense of a true good, but it is a common good in the sense of an ordinary good. Let us imagine that a group of people buy a house and each contributes an equal share of money. To all of them the house will be a common good. However, although a common good, the house is not a moral good. As it satisfies everyone's desire for shelter, it is an ordinary good.

3.6   The common good in the second sense: as a society of equals

We have seen that Green uses the common good in the meaning of the process of moral growth. Additionally, he speaks of the common good in terms of some 'common end' which all individuals should unitedly pursue.[44] In more abstract terms this common end is described as 'a spiritual activity in which all may partake, and in which all must partake, if it is to amount to a full realisation of the faculties of the human soul'.[45] In more concrete terms the common end is a type of society where all men are equal, it is a 'development of society into a state in which all human beings shall be treated as, actually or in promise, persons – as agents of whom each is an end equally to himself and to others'.[46] The second sense of Green's common good is based on a particular vision of justice and happiness. Here the common good is not a spiritual or altruistic activity in which an individual can find self-fulfilment. It is clearly seen as a form of social life:

> It [the ultimate good] must be a perfecting of *man* – not of any human faculty in abstraction, or of any imaginary individuals in that detachment from social relations in which they would not be men at all. We are therefore justified in holding that it could not be attained in a life of mere scientific and artistic activity, any more than in one of 'practical' exertion from which those activities were absent; *in holding further that the life in which it is attained must be a social life, in which all men freely and consciously co-operate …*[47]

The 'common good' comes to express Green's vision of how the perfecting of the individual soul should be achieved in practical, social terms. Although Green claims that the ideal of the ultimate good is abstract and that we can discover its concrete content only in the process of its unfolding, he asserts that the common end is a particular type of society with particular institutions. We should understand the true end of our human moral effort 'not as determined merely by an abstract idea of law, but as implying (what it must in fact imply) a whole world of beneficent social activities'.[48]

What I call the second sense of the common good Simhony takes to be its main meaning. She argues persuasively that Green's common good 'is about a certain kind of society, social union which both underpins relation of mutual interest and gives it effect'.[49] I believe that this is a legitimate interpretation of the common good and, as Simhony shows, it offers solutions to difficult practical dilemmas and answers to unfair criticisms of Green.

I argue that the first and the second senses of the common good differ in an essential way. The common good as the effort of seeking one's own good in conjunction with the good of others is different from the common good as the society of equals which is the only means through which the human soul can perfect itself. In the first sense, the common good is a principle of moral action. The objects in which it can find expression can be sought and achieved only by an agent exerting moral effort. The common good as a moral good is exclusively related to a particular person. Each individual should seek her own 'common good'. She should find out for herself the object in which her true good resides. As can be seen in the first sense of the common good, the use of the term 'common' is very specific. The common good is common as a result but personal as an aspiration, as an effort, as an act of self-fulfilment.

The common good as the society of equals is common in a different way. Although Green attempts to present his idea of the just society as a development of that vein of thought which has already introduced the common good as the moral ideal, his message departs from its starting point. In other words, although he presents the equal society as a moral objective in the pursuit of which the individuals can seek fulfilment, this does not express the full value of social equality. The just society is not a moral good. Its 'goodness' cannot be seen primarily as that of a moral achievement. When Green describes the value of social equality he may emphasise the moral effort involved in its attainment; however, he places much stronger emphasis on the benefits this equality will bring to the general improvement of humankind. Social equality is good to all in common and to all alike. It is not good because it could be someone's self-fulfilment: its value does not consist in its being a moral ideal. For individuals the good society is an ordinary good, not a moral good. It aims to satisfy a person as a private self, not as an extended common self – the self which one acquires only within a moral act. The ordinary good is a good which is meant to be good for oneself – not to the exclusion of others, but not necessarily to their inclusion. According to Green's definition, in the perfect society everyone is treated as an end: each person is valued simply on account of his human nature. This implies that everyone deserves social welfare and justice regardless of whether they act as moral agents or not.

Green's just society is 'commonly' good to all. All are recipients of its goodness. To those who contribute to its creation in a moral way – by means of overcoming their personal inclinations – the just society is both an ordinary and a moral good. However, the exclusive value of the social equality is its unrivalled capacity to provide ordinary good: in Green's estimation, it can provide more good than any other social formation or human artefact at all. [50]

3.7   Conclusion

Analysing in turn Green's moral theory preceding the introduction of the common good (Chapter 2) and his common good theory leads to the conclusion that a particular object is morally good only with respect to the person who has produced it. The same object is ordinarily good to those who benefit from it. If the common good is understood only in its substantive sense, that is, as a particular object that is good to many people in common, then it represents an ordinary, not a moral good. Green would not have been satisfied with a concept of the common good that does not reflect the moral character of the individual. That is why, I believe, the substantive version of the common good on its own does not render the fullness of his common good theory.

The overall tone of this chapter has been rather critical. I have accused Green of failing to spell out the two meanings of the common good; failing to state explicitly that the theory of the common good reflects a process of moral growth; and failing to maintain the distinction between ordinary and moral good. However, as I mentioned at the outset, my purpose has been to restate Green's common good theory in such a way that it reveals its enormous strength. One of its main assets is that it discloses the genealogy of moral motivation. Green shows us that we pursue the moral good because we find ordinary good insufficient. We are looking for a good that is permanent and find this permanency in some form of a social bond. The moral good does not imply self-denial, but rather self-enlightenment. If we discover it and pursue it, we achieve a higher degree of self-satisfaction. Green presents us with the phenomenology of moral motivation and thus offers us a philosophically interesting concept of moral behaviour. Green's common good theory shows us that moral conduct entails a process of self-transcendence, a process of overcoming one's narrowly personal vision and interest. This is the connection between Green's moral philosophy and Husserl's phenomenology. While for Husserl, some self-transformation is inherent in attaining a scientific standpoint, for Green, this self-transformation is the key element of moral conduct.[51]

The reason why Green does not underline the difference between the personal good and the common good (or between the ordinary good and the moral good) is because he wants to show us the level at which these two coincide. However, acknowledging the difference between the ordinary and the moral good should not necessarily damage the idea of the common good. There are at least two reasons why this difference has to be accounted for. First, one could not be in a position to pursue the common good unless others cared for themselves, that is, unless they needed ordinary goods. Secondly, moral acts would not be an achievement unless they involved a degree of overcoming of one's self-perception of oneself as an absolute end.

The idea that the theory of the common good represents an attempt to define the nature of morality is very clearly presented in Green's theory of human rights in *Lectures on the Principles of Political Obligation*. There he argues that 'the moral personality – the capacity on the part of an individual for making a common good his own – ought to be developed; and it is developed through rights'.[52] However, most of Green's readers draw their knowledge of the common good theory from the *Prolegomena*, which may leave the impression that Green misinterprets human nature by assuming that everybody has a noble social interest and always sees his private well-being in the light of the common good.

4
Positive and Negative Freedom: Green's Contribution to the Debate[1]

The debate on positive and negative freedom has been part of the political theory agenda for quite a long time now.[2] It is one of these issues about which different political theorists hold very strong views and little can be done to change one's commitment to either kind of freedom, or one's belief that this debate is fruitless. Recently, the concept of republican freedom[3] has been gathering more popularity as an alternative to the positive/negative freedom debate. After defending Green's philosophy of freedom from many of the attacks it has received, Peter Nicholson concludes that 'the dichotomy between negative freedom and positive freedom cannot be applied to Green's theory'. He says that this debate is 'a Procrustean bed, and laying Green's theory on it leaves it truncated and bleeding away its vitality'.[4] The insights of Green's concept of freedom are only diminished when this concept is taken out of its context and then forced to represent only one side of what is believed to be the full nature of freedom. As I believe Nicholson's conclusion is largely justified, I need to have very good reasons to re-open the debate and make Green part of it.

The reason is the following. I argue that the relation between positive and negative freedom, on analysis, exemplifies the dialectic between moral good and ordinary good which was discussed in Chapter 3. Further, the negative and positive understandings of freedom also represent the two perspectives of defining the moral good, discussed in Chapter 2. The current positive/negative freedom debate can make us look again at Green's theory of freedom and bring out ideas that can advance this debate. In other words, against the background of the debate, Green's theory can receive new vitality as it has the potential to address issues that are seen as important in contemporary political philosophy. This is my aim in this chapter: to remind readers of, reinterpret and develop Green's philosophical analysis of freedom, and use this analysis as a foundation to make claims that go beyond what Green maintained himself.

Green's philosophy of freedom leads us to see that the two usages of freedom in the realm of the political are underpinned by the two different senses of freedom in the realm of personal experience, which Green calls the *juristic* and the *true* sense of freedom. The distinction between true and juristic freedom in the personal sphere is similar but not identical to the distinction between positive and negative freedom in the political sphere. Both distinctions are instances of a more general relationship between ordinary good and moral good. However, the nature of this relationship changes as we move from the personal to the political sphere, because political action necessarily involves interaction between agents.

It has been argued, successfully, that the difference between positive and negative freedom should not be seen as based on the standard distinction, as set out by Berlin, between negative freedom *from* obstacles and positive freedom *to* achieve goals.[5] On my view, the dichotomy can be maintained, but explained in a different way. Tom Baldwin, for example, argues that the defenders of positive freedom expound beliefs that can be summed by the doctrine of 'ethical naturalism', while this is not the case with the defenders of negative freedom.[6] However, Berlin's concept of negative liberty does imply a view of human nature that is not far from ethical naturalism. Many philosophers have argued that negative freedom is not as morally neutral as its defenders claim it is.[7] Therefore, it is not necessarily true that the two concepts imply two different understandings of human nature. I offer a new distinction which reaches the somewhat trivial conclusion that both forms of freedom are mutually dependent and equally valuable. However, I believe that I advance an idea that has not been argued before – that the two kinds of freedom reflect the two aspects of our moral nature. The formal distinction I shall be proposing for the purpose of expressing this dichotomy better is between negative freedom *received* by the agent and positive freedom *gained* in the act of helping others.

One of the main ideas advanced here is that the dual usage of freedom is a matter of necessity. I argue that the division between positive and negative freedom in the political context is underpinned by a related division in the personal sphere, between what Green calls 'true' (and I will refer to as 'moral') and 'juristic' freedoms. That is why the conclusions of this chapter enter into disagreement with three parties: those who defend positive freedom at the expense of negative freedom, those who defend negative freedom at the expense of positive freedom; and those (like MacCallum) who reject the distinction between positive and negative freedom.[8] The chapter does not aim to synthesise the two concepts of freedom into a single overarching concept, as Philip Pettit and other modern defenders of republicanism have recently attempted to do with the concept of 'republican freedom'.[9] I argue that a suitably refined distinction between positive and negative freedom presents a true dichotomy, and that the polarity between them should be kept and explained rather than rejected.

Another concern of this chapter is to demonstrate that although the two conceptual couples of 'juristic and moral' and 'negative and positive' freedoms correspond to each other, they do not overlap. While moral freedom is more complex than the juristic one, negative freedom is more complex than positive freedom. These conclusions go against the following misconceptions: first, that the negative understanding of freedom is more straightforward and morally neutral, and secondly, that the notion of positive freedom carries, in some latent form, totalitarian thrusts. By revealing the interconnection between positive and negative freedoms, this chapter brings forward the positive political values inherent to both of them.

The discussion of the relation between positive and negative freedom is preceded by an analysis of moral and juristic freedom. This gives us the opportunity to explore the changes in the meaning of freedom in the context of general human practice and to gain grounds for explaining positive and negative freedom. The core philosophical theme of the chapter is that both the divisions between juristic and moral freedoms on the one side, and negative and positive freedoms on the other, are underpinned by the relationship between ordinary and moral good. I have argued in

Chapter 3 that what stands as moral good in relation to the agent who produces it, stands as ordinary good in relation to the person who consumes it. Applied to the issue of freedom: what is a moral freedom to the agent who has achieved some self-fulfilment translates as juristic freedom to those who benefit from the agent's conduct. The relation between positive and negative freedoms is similar: the agent of positive freedom acts as a producer, while the agent of negative freedom is a recipient of goods. However, because the concepts of positive and negative freedoms emerge in the context of social life, there are differences between the two conceptual couples. Moral freedom corresponds to positive freedom, but while the former focuses on the nature of self-fulfilment, the latter deals with issues of social justice and equality. Finally, the chapter addresses the issue about which freedom is the most important. Here I argue that the evaluation of freedom should depend on the perspective from which it is performed. A moral agent reaches one conclusion (about which freedom is more important) when her own freedom is concerned and another conclusion when she has to decide for somebody else.

4.1 Juristic freedom and moral freedom

Green offers two analyses of freedom, one in the general context of all human behaviour, the other in the more specific context of political behaviour. While in the first context (as developed in his theory of the will) he discusses two different senses of freedom – the 'juristic' and the 'true' (the moral) sense – in the second context (in his political theory) he develops only the notion of 'positive' freedom by analogy with 'moral' freedom. As Green does not develop the distinction between positive and negative freedom in the political sphere, he also does not explore the parallels between these four interrelated concepts. This chapter aims to reconcile these two analyses and on the basis of this juxtaposition, to extract more from Green's philosophy. Green's claim that we use 'freedom' in different senses – a claim that is analysed at length in this section – gives us grounds to argue that the notion of positive freedom is not sufficient to account fully for the entire phenomenon of freedom. Understanding the distinction which Green introduces between juristic and the moral freedom will lead to conclusions that go beyond what the British idealist argued himself (and what he is famous for) and will bring a new dimension to the debate on positive and negative freedom.

This section addresses two issues. First, it explains why we, by necessity, use 'freedom' in different senses. Secondly, it discusses the relation between juristic and moral freedom by exploring why Green has chosen these two types of freedom; why they are generically different; why Green believes that moral freedom is more important, and whether he is right.

Green's two analyses of freedom are to be found in his two major essays on freedom, both delivered as lectures. In the first, 'On the Different Senses of "Freedom" as Applied to Will and the Moral Progress of Man',[10] he analyses the meaning of personal freedom in the context of his theory of the will as developed in his *Prolegomena to Ethics*. In the second, 'Lecture on "Liberal Legislation and Freedom of Contract"', Green discusses freedom in the political realm and explains its implications for social practice.[11] I will now address the first of these lectures, and subsequently, in section 4.2, the second.

4.1.1 Freedom and the nature of human agency

In the first of his lectures (hereafter referred to as *Freedom*), Green investigates two major senses in which the word 'freedom' is used. One of them is the 'primary' or the 'juristic' sense, which is 'freedom as exemption from external control'.[12] The second is the 'true' or 'real' freedom, which can be understood as 'the goal of moral endeavour',[13] as 'devotion to self-imposed duties'.[14] I shall use the term 'moral' freedom to represent Green's concept of 'true' freedom. Green believes that our notions of freedom progress naturally from the 'juristic' towards the 'moral'. Our pursuit of freedom starts as a desire to break through any external limitation to what we may like to do, and tends to develop into a pursuit of a higher self, of a true self-fulfilment. The theory which Green develops in order to explain this transformation of juristic into moral freedom is, in essence, a restatement of his theory of the will as developed in Book II of *Prolegomena*, and discussed here in Chapter 1.

Green establishes a connection between freedom and the will. According to him, willing is already an exercise of freedom. In the opening paragraph of his lecture he claims: 'the will is always free – or more properly ... a man in willing is necessarily free, since willing constitutes freedom, and "free will" is a pleonasm = "free freedom" ...'.[15] We are capable of being free because we are willing agents. We want things and we need freedom in order to attain them. Green's idea is that the phenomenon of freedom is embedded in the human capacity to will; that one's concept of freedom is based on one's understanding of what is good.

Green's theory of the will can be used to explain why what is good for us changes. It changes precisely because the pursuit of the good is mediated by one's notion of what this good is; the good is never inextricably attached to the same object. A person's idea of his own self-satisfaction develops because, as a result of ever-growing experience, his vision of what is good expands. The attainment of one good widens his horizon for other goods, that is why his notion of the good develops.[16] Green believes it develops towards an idea of 'permanent good' and this good is to be found in moral conduct.[17] In the same manner, the meaning of freedom to an individual changes over time, and from one set of circumstances to another, by reflecting the changes in one's notion of what is good.

Now we are in a position to see that the fluctuation of the meaning of freedom derives from the nature of human agency. According to Green's theory of the will, a person's behaviour is characterised by his pursuit of an object with which he identifies himself. The content of this object is permanently renewed as his idea of what is good for him constantly progresses. The concept of freedom, as well as the concept of good, is subject to permanent development; 'the nature of the freedom really differs according to the nature of the object which the man makes his own, or with which he identifies himself'.[18] The meaning of freedom becomes clear only when it is placed in the context of personal experience – we are free when we fulfil the object of our will. Freedom is much more importantly defined as 'a pursuit of a particular self-satisfaction', rather than as 'an alleviation of restrictions'. There are many examples showing that absence of restrictions does not amount to freedom, unless these are restrictions to someone's pursuit of self-satisfaction.[19]

The fluctuation of the concept of freedom is essential as it reflects the nature of personal experience. In the same manner in which one's concept of good tends to progress towards a 'permanent good', the pursuit of freedom advances towards a concept of 'permanent' freedom which is no longer 'to do as I like', but to get involved in a pursuit of a common good. Green's argument in *Freedom* shows that our conception of freedom *necessarily* departs from its juristic starting point.

The moral sense of freedom reflects each person's necessity to overcome the insufficiencies of his transient individual existence. Green associates himself with 'the Stoics, St Paul, Kant and Hegel' and shares with them 'the view which underlies all theories implying that freedom is in some sense the goal of moral endeavour, the view, namely, that there is some true will in a man with which many or most of his voluntary actions do not accord, a higher self that is not satisfied by the objects which yet he deliberately pursues'.[20]

Let us now address the issue of why Green has chosen these two particular senses of freedom and why he believes that moral freedom differs substantially from the juristic one. He claims that both freedoms lead to a feeling of self-satisfaction as they both represent 'an achievement of the self-seeking principle'.[21] So juristic and moral freedoms have a common root – the will of the agent. They are both freedoms to act as one wants to – even if a person decides to do 'as she should', that is, to be 'truly' free, she is still acting on her own will. The important difference is the following. Having attained juristic freedom, an agent looks for something more, for a freedom of a new kind. Juristic freedom 'is a form of self-enjoyment' Green claims, 'which consists essentially in the feeling by the subject of a possibility rather than a reality, of what it has it in itself to become, not of what it actually is'.[22]

MacCallum has famously argued that the debate about different kinds of freedom is 'unrewarding' because all allegedly different types of freedom can be subsumed under a single formal definition.[23] His definition discloses freedom as 'triadic relation' between agents, constraints and actions.[24] According to MacCallum's theory the difference between juristic and moral freedom cannot reflect a genuine distinction between two kinds of freedom, but can only emphasise two different aspects of what is the same phenomenon. Baldwin and Nicholson have argued that MacCallum's 'generic schema of freedom' manages to account for Green's concept of juristic freedom but fails to apply for the concept of moral or real freedom.[25] Nicholson argues that while juristic freedom denotes an area where the individual is given the opportunity to act as he chooses, real freedom 'is a moral concept and denotes the individual's doing, or having a character which is disposed to do, what is morally right'. That is why there is 'a fundamental difference between the two senses of freedom independent of their identity of form'.[26]

One way to give a more formal account of the distinction between juristic and moral freedom is to argue that the two freedoms reflect the pursuit of the two types of good: ordinary and moral. We can argue that in doing 'what we like' and in doing 'what we should' we are satisfying two different needs. The first is the spontaneous need to pursue an object to our own satisfaction, the second is the need to achieve something beyond the boundary of the conventional, to achieve self-mastery, to act as a moral agent. The understanding of the distinction between juristic and moral freedom can boil down to explaining the difference between ordinary good and moral good. The difference between juristic and moral freedom is to be seen in the different nature of the objects that are being pursued by the free agent. When one is free 'to do as he likes' the object of his pursuit is the ordinary good; when she is free because she 'is acting as she should' the object of her pursuit is the moral good. This formal criterion for distinguishing between moral and juristic freedom (linking them, respectively, to the moral and the ordinary good) will be helpful for the analysis of the relation between the two kinds of freedom.

4.1.2 The relation between juristic and moral freedoms, or the dialectic of ordinary and moral good

Understanding the relation between juristic and moral freedoms is very important for several reasons. It carries implications for the debate on positive and negative freedoms and it will give us the method for comparing different freedoms. It is also important because Green leaves the analysis of this relation philosophically incomplete. Although he makes many improvements on the interpretation of this relation inherited from his predecessors (Stoics, St Paul, Kant and Hegel), he leaves one question without a satisfactory answer. Is juristic freedom valuable in itself? Thus he leaves to his critics the possibility to draw their own conclusions.

We know for sure that Green does not pull juristic and moral freedoms so far apart from each other that they come to represent two opposite things. For him, they represent stages in the development of a person. One's will is the common element to both these senses of freedom. Green criticises Kant for 'the notion of there being two wills or selves in a man, the "pure" will or ego and the "empirical" will or ego – the pure will being independent of a man's actual desires and directed to the fulfilment of a universal law of which it is itself the giver, the empirical will being determined by the strongest desire and directed to this or that pleasure'.[27] Green's view is that, although Kant's terminology makes sense, 'it must be borne in mind that the pure and empirical egos are still not two egos but one ego; the "pure ego" being the self-realising principle considered with reference to ... its idea, its possibility, what it has in itself to become ...; the "empirical ego" being the same principle as it appears in this or that state of character, ... but does not represent that which it has in itself to become ...'[28] According to Green, moral and juristic freedoms represent two different stages in the development of human spirit.

Green could deal easily with an accusation that his freedom theory neglects the importance of juristic freedom. For Green, the exercise of juristic freedom is a necessary step in the process of building the character that enables you to exercise moral freedom. The latter is not about forbidding yourself to desire the 'wrong things', but about cultivating the will to do the 'right things'. This can only happen if one has juristic freedom to start with. Nicholson points out that, in the context of Green's freedom theory, the loss of juristic freedom 'would matter greatly'.[29]

However, the question whether juristic freedom is valuable in itself remains. So far it is clear that Green does not neglect its importance. It is also clear, though, that he prioritises moral freedom over juristic freedom. The logic of this priority is the same as that of the moral good over ordinary good. Green's belief that, in some important way, the moral good supersedes the ordinary good, was discussed in section 3.5. The attainment of the moral good implies overcoming one's natural impulses for the purpose of achieving deeper and truer self-fulfilment. The highest stage of the moral progress is expressed in 'the growth of a personal interest in ... doing what is believed to contribute to the absolutely desirable or to human perfection'.[30] The moral good combines two aspects: it marks the attainment of the deepest form of self-fulfilment and it is directed towards the common good.

Green prioritises moral freedom over juristic freedom in the same way in which he prioritises moral good over ordinary good. I argue, however, that this priority is conditional, not absolute, and that Green is wrong to take it to the point where he practically denies the status of ordinary good as being good at all. In the previous chapter I have demonstrated that moral good is impossible without ordinary good. As the relation between moral freedom and juristic freedom is based on the same principle as the relation between moral and ordinary good, the same argument will be applicable now: juristic freedom is not only a stepping stone towards the attainment of moral freedom, but an essential element of its constitution.

The argument in section 3.5 was that attainment of the moral good is impossible without the parallel existence of the ordinary good. One's moral good translates as another's ordinary good. To the recipients of my production of good, the good I produce is ordinary. It is meant to satisfy them not as part of a wider community, but as ends to themselves. For me, my production of good to others is the true good, because it is meant to satisfy me not as a sole subject, but as a subject who has identified herself with others.

When we apply this argument to our discussion on juristic and moral freedom, we reach the conclusion that we could not exercise moral freedom unless juristic freedom also existed. We cannot be truly free by acting as moral agents unless other people needed ordinary good, that is, exercised their freedom in a juristic sense. We cannot liberate others if they do not need to be liberated. A moral action always has an agent and a recipient. While, for the agent, the good he produces is a moral good – it satisfies a moral need – for the recipient the produced good is an ordinary good as it satisfies an ordinary need.

To conclude: this section has explicated Green's argument that we use 'freedom' in different senses as a matter of course. The nature of human agency is such that our notion of freedom changes with the development of our notion of good. The difference between moral and juristic freedoms reflects the difference between moral and ordinary good. As Green considers the pursuit of moral good to be superior to that of ordinary good, he also prioritises moral freedom over juristic freedom. However, just as Green has 'lost' the concept of the ordinary good, he has left open the question about the status of juristic freedom. In Chapter 3, I argued that a self-centred disposition can never be absolutely overcome. Moral conduct always implies a recipient who, at the time, is not acting as a moral agent. In the same way, moral freedom cannot be exercised unless someone needs juristic freedom. There can be occasions when juristic freedom is an end in itself, not a stepping stone towards higher forms of freedom. The dialectic of the relation between moral and ordinary good applies to that of moral and juristic freedoms. This dialectic leads to the conclusion that both kinds of freedom can be ends in themselves. Can we legitimately prioritise one over the other? I will return to this question at the end of this chapter.

4.2 Positive freedom and negative freedom

I have mentioned that Green speaks about two senses of freedom in the realm of personal experience, yet he develops only the notion of positive freedom in the realm of political practice. The lack of a formal account, as well as the lack of defence, of a concept of negative freedom constitutes a gap in Green's political philosophy. I argue that Isaiah Berlin fills this gap by developing a case for negative freedom in his paper 'Two Concepts of Liberty'. However, neither Green, who defends positive freedom, nor Berlin, who defends negative freedom, sees his concepts of freedom as only the one side of a necessary conceptual couple. In other words, it is not only Green who does not see that by omitting the notion of negative freedom he leaves the analysis of political freedom incomplete. Berlin also is unaware of the extent to which his defence of negative freedom rests on the concept, and relies on the practice, of positive freedom. This section offers a formal scheme for defining positive and negative freedom in a way that clearly demonstrates the difference between them, and at the same time reveals their interdependence. One of my aims is to explain that the distinction between juristic and moral freedom underpins (although it does not fully overlap) the distinction between negative and positive freedom.

This section adopts the following strategy. I take Green's concept of positive freedom and Berlin's concept of negative freedom to be the archetypes, so I analyse them in turn. I explain why Green's concept of positive freedom diverges from his notion of moral freedom and on this basis I explain why Berlin's famous criticism of positive freedom fails to apply in Green's case. Further, I elucidate Berlin's negative freedom by offering a definition that spells out its full complexity. This definition reveals that negative and positive freedom are not only antagonistic to each other (as it is Berlin's aim to prove), but also interconnected. I address the issue about which of the two freedoms is more important in the third and final section of this chapter.

4.2.1   Positive freedom

Green's discussion of positive freedom is introduced in a different context from his discussion of juristic and moral freedoms. Green's second lecture on freedom (hereafter, *Liberal Legislation*) discusses the meaning of liberty in the context of deliberating its social practice. Thus we shall see that although the concept of positive freedom corresponds to that of moral freedom, the former differs from the latter as it explicitly emphasises the fact that the exercise of freedom takes place as a relation between individuals in a social context.

For Green 'freedom in the positive sense' is 'the liberation of the powers of all men equally for contributions to a common good'.[31] This is positive freedom because it is constructive, its exercise contributes to the well-being of others. Nicholson points out that the concept of positive freedom corresponds to Green's 'true freedom'.[32] Green wants to emphasise that we should see freedom in terms of moral action rather than as an unobstructed pursuit of enjoyment. However, in *Liberal Legislation*, Green's defence of moral action has shifted emphasis from the 'self-perfection' aspect towards acting for a common good. Before I explain Green's concept of positive freedom further, I will briefly address Berlin's criticism of it.

Our general knowledge of positive freedom is formed, to a large extent, by Berlin's shrewd analysis of, and vigorous attack on, this concept. According to Berlin, positive freedom is a pursuit of self-mastery and it is based on a metaphysical split in the personality into a lower, 'heteronomous' self, on the one side, and a higher, 'ideal', 'autonomous' self, on the other.[33] He argues that, for the exponents of positive freedom, a person should try to achieve her ideal (autonomous) self and should suppress her lower (empirical) self. Further to that, Berlin believes that someone could use the division between the true and the empirical self as a ground to *force others* to pursue their higher and perfect selves. The appeal to self-mastery on a personal level may transfer to a public imposition of certain ways of life. It was pointed out earlier that Green disagrees with Kant that we can speak about two selves or two egos. However, provided it is properly defined, Green accepts the distinction between the 'empirical ego' and the 'pure ego'.[34] It almost seems that Berlin's argument strikes Green's freedom theory at its heart.

The reason why this is not so is that the transfer of commendation for inner self-mastery to public enforcement of such self-mastery does not occur in Green's political philosophy.[35] The concept of positive freedom is based on that of moral freedom, but analyses the meaning of freedom in a political context and thus brings forward new considerations. Once the concept of freedom is immersed in a political context, Green's emphasis shifts from explaining what true self-fulfilment is and how important it is to the individual, to explaining how those deprived of recourses for self-fulfilment can gain access to them. So the concept of positive freedom is based on the awareness that the amount of basic (juristic) freedom we have depends on existing social arrangements.

The concept of positive freedom developed in *Liberal Legislation* goes together with a social analysis of the access different people have to freedom. Green explains that no individual's freedom would exist in practice unless society acted unanimously and this unanimous action were directed towards enabling people to exercise their powers. Freedom has to be actively provided and created by people's involvement in positive action. Green points out that the 'alleviation of restrictions' does not imply abstinence from action on behalf of society or government; on the contrary, it implies active involvement in producing legislation and institutions that will protect the individual's freedom. His point is that individuals will enjoy freedom only if someone protects and guarantees this freedom.

4.2.2 The context in which Green explains positive freedom

In *Liberal Legislation* Green discusses and defends a new wave of liberal legislation introduced after 1868 regulating employment, education, liquor traffic and land transactions. The Employers'

Liability Act, for example, introduced limits on 'the conditions under which certain kinds of labour may be bought and sold'.[36] Green believed that the new liberal legislation was a step along the road of political reform aiming to further 'social good against class interests'.[37] However, the new liberal legislation met a lot of resistance as some claimed that '[i]n certain respects it has put restraints on the individual in doing what he will with his own'.[38] Elements of this argument against the legislation limiting the freedom of contract can be discerned in Lord Bradbourne's speech to the House of Lords given on 24 August 1880.[39] The argument, briefly presented by Green, is the following:

> 'The workman,' it was argued, 'should be left to take care of himself by the terms of his agreement with the employer. It is not for the state to step in and say, as by the new act it says, that when a workman is hurt in carrying out the instructions of the employer or his foreman, the employer, in the absence of a special agreement to the contrary, shall be liable for compensation. If the law thus takes to protecting men, whether tenant-farmers, or pitmen, or railway servants, who ought to be able to protect themselves, it tends to weaken their self-reliance, and thus, in unwisely seeking to do them good, it lowers them in the scale of moral beings.'[40]

Green's lecture shows that the expressed view is either hypocritical or short-sighted. This old liberal defence of the idea of state non-intervention leads Green to analyse the meaning of freedom. He observes that the value of freedom changes according to the circumstances of the agent who possesses it. If there were full freedom of contract in the employment of labour in the conditions of late Victorian society, would this freedom be equally good to all parties of the contract? It would clearly be beneficial to the employers – it would give them the opportunity to buy labour at its cheapest. But to the workers or farm labourers who have no bargaining power, this freedom of contract would be 'an instrument of disguised oppression'.[41] So if freedom offers ever greater chances for the pursuit of happiness while, at the same time, it deprives others of such opportunities, then freedom for freedom's sake becomes a socially untenable project.

Freedom when 'rightly understood' should not be seen as 'merely freedom from restraint and compulsion' or 'merely freedom to do as we like irrespective of what it is that we like'.[42] Freedom can be socially desirable when it is 'a positive power or capacity of doing or enjoying something worth doing and enjoying, and that, too, something that we do or enjoy in common with others'.[43] It is very important to read Green's philosophical message bearing in mind the context of his political polemics. When he says that 'to submit is the first step to true freedom',[44] he is not implying that people should give up their personal happiness in the pursuit of the common good. His appeal for a positive exercise of freedom translates differently depending on one's particular social circumstances. When Green claims that the exercise of freedom has to entail a commitment to social welfare, his appeal has a particular addressee: those who already possess the social facilities for self-improvement. It is their capacities for self-fulfilment that, Green believes, *should* be employed in creating a project where their good is united to the good of the others. Those who benefit most from societal life should pursue altruistic projects rather than their own self-fulfilment, exclusively. To the workers and farm labourers the new liberal legislation is not an appeal for altruistic behaviour or the sacrifice of ordinary pleasures; it serves them as a 'powerful friend', as it aims to increase their access to basic goods.[45]

The main conclusion of Green's lecture on *Liberal Legislation* is that the value of freedom depends on the social arrangements that we, as a society, have achieved. The understanding of freedom can never be fully detached from the pursuit of justice and equality – a separation which the defenders of negative freedom believe possible. We can avoid the scenario where one's freedom is at the same time someone else's oppression only if we share the belief in the value of the human individual, a belief that everyone's fulfilment has equal worth. As a society we need to accept some form of legislation and obey it voluntarily, otherwise freedom will be abused under one form or another.

The concept of positive freedom rests on the concept of moral freedom, but diverges from it to the extent that the former is immersed in a political context. While the weight of moral freedom is to be found in the ultimate self-fulfilment of an individual (whilst implying his self-fulfilment has a social character), the weight of positive freedom is to be seen in the fact that the free agent is a voluntary contributor to a common good (whilst implying that only in this way can she be truly self-fulfilled). Berlin rejects positive freedom on the basis of the observation that if the austerity of an individual's moral perfection, that is, of moral freedom, is being transferred from the realm of private life to the sphere of the political life, then the result is an atrocious violation of human rights. Green's concept of positive freedom resists such an accusation.

Green's defence of positive freedom suggests a formal definition of positive freedom which simultaneously explains its difference from negative freedom and its relation to it. In the case of positive freedom, the agent fulfils his freedom in his capacity as a 'producer' of moral goods; in the case of negative freedom, the agent is a 'recipient' of such goods. As there are necessarily two sides to each moral interaction – productive and recipient counterparts – political freedom has its two aspects – positive and negative. Trying to explain the difference between positive and negative freedom on the basis of the distinction 'from/to' has proved unsatisfactory – a case argued by MacCallum.[46] Unlike MacCallum who wants to obliterate this distinction altogether, I believe that we can speak of two defensible cases of freedom in the sphere of both personal experience and public life. The definition of a positively free agent as a producer of good and of a negatively free agent as a recipient of moral treatment captures the intentions of Berlin's 'from/to' division but overcomes its weaknesses.

I, like many others, find Green's theory of positive freedom persuasive. If it were open to any criticism, it would be that it leaves a gap: he does not develop the concept of negative freedom. In the next chapter I argue that Green's theory of human rights is, on analysis, a defence of negative freedom. None the less, he fails to present this defence in an explicit form. This is what Isaiah Berlin does.

4.2.3   Berlin's negative freedom

Berlin believes that a genuine understanding of freedom is represented by the 'negative' concept of liberty. Freedom should not be seen as self-mastery, but rather in its more basic and straightforward sense of 'warding off interference'.[47] His defence of negative freedom is far from simplistic or socially naive. Berlin differs from Green's opponents in *Liberal Legislation* who insist on state noninterference without taking into account its practical social implications. He realises that the meaning and the importance of freedom vary in different social contexts. He takes into account the possibility that under conditions of hardship or of grievous social inequality, an individual may voluntarily give up his juristic freedom if this will redress social injustice. 'I can,' claims Berlin, 'like the Russian critic Belinsky, say that if others are to be deprived of it – if my brothers are to remain in poverty, squalor and chains – then I do not want it for myself, I reject it with both hands and infinitely prefer to share their fate.'[48] Berlin admits that the evaluation of one's own juristic freedom depends on the social environment in which this freedom is exercised. However, he goes on to make an important claim. Even if under some social conditions one's juristic freedom is unsustainable, it does not mean that this freedom has to be perpetually sacrificed. Whenever a person is forced to give up her freedom to do as she likes, 'an absolute loss of liberty occurs'.[49] Ideally, nobody should have to sacrifice their freedom, because sacrificing freedom is a loss of personal happiness and therefore a loss of humanity. Berlin insists that among the many different and complex understandings of freedom we should choose one, the most basic one. We should understand liberty as 'liberty *from*', as 'absence of interference beyond the shifting, but always recognisable, frontier'.[50]

Thus, initially, Berlin acknowledges the defence of positive freedom. He understands why it is impossible to dissociate freedom from the phenomena of social justice and equality. However, he argues that the authentic meaning of freedom is to be seen as the opposite of positive freedom, as 'the "negative" goal of warding off interference'.[51] Although Berlin grasps the logic of understanding liberty as a commitment to social welfare, he still argues that this misrepresents its meaning.

Berlin develops a powerful message but falls short of expressing it in clear, formal terms. The achievement of his theory of negative liberty is that it does not fully negate the notion of positive freedom, but goes beyond it. His insight is that besides positive freedom, there exists another freedom – a negative one – and the significance of the latter has been unduly undermined. The value of negative freedom can be seen only when we grasp the limitations and shortcomings of positive freedom. That is why, I believe, it is very important to see that Berlin's definition of negative freedom captures the extent to which he also accepts positive freedom. The definition which he fails to give, but perhaps should have given, is the following: the concept of negative freedom renders the understanding that although the individual can enjoy freedom only as a member of a society which protects her rights (which is what Green believes to be the case), *she is still not obliged to commit herself fully to a reciprocal service to this society*. A 'frontier must be drawn' between her obligations to society and her obligations to herself as a human individual.[52] By expressing Berlin's point in this way we can see two things: first, Berlin has developed a new meaning of freedom, different from the positive one – a meaning that Green does not develop in his political theory; and secondly, we can see that the definition of negative freedom derives from the definition of positive freedom.

Berlin's concept of negative liberty expresses a political vision of how proper legislation would work for the purpose of protecting the individual's juristic freedom. His idea of a 'shifting, but always recognisable frontier' beyond which there should be no interference is in essence an idea about a recognised social arrangement concerning the sphere of an individual's liberty.[53] However, social arrangements function properly only in a society whose members act as citizens, that is, exercise positive freedom. Berlin's message is that even though there is no proper personal freedom outside society, the individual is entitled to have a space in which what they do is irrelevant to the moral concerns of that society.

Negative freedom is the individual's entitlement to reject moral claims made on her by society, while this society, none the less, does provide services protecting her rights. Negative freedom is about the individual's entitlement to be a recipient of social care. This definition clearly demonstrates that negative freedom is only possible in conjunction with positive freedom. One can be a recipient of social care only if somebody is prepared to provide it. Individuals, as members of a society, should be ready to allow each other, in Berlin's words, 'a minimum area of personal freedom'.[54] His point is that the individual is not only a citizen; that he should not be seen only as a dutiful agent but that *he should also be entitled to be released from moral obligations*. I find this appeal justified. What I will add is that a person can release her fellow human beings from a moral obligation, but the very act of such release is a moral act. In essence, Berlin's defence of negative freedom is an appeal for moral action of a more complex nature. If I allow somebody the space to pursue his private interests, that is, if I give him the freedom to choose not to act morally, I am acting out of a moral disposition, that is, as a positively free agent.

The distinction between positive and negative freedom arises in a social context as it reveals the recognition that our freedom is limited or enhanced by our social partners. This distinction depends on who performs the liberation – the agent who seeks freedom, or his fellow human beings. Positive freedom is exercised by the person who participates actively in the process of alleviating hindrances. A person exercises negative freedom as a recipient of someone else's effort to remove restrictions. The distinction between positive and negative freedom defines whether the individual is a performer or a recipient *of moral action*. Relatedness to moral behaviour is important for both these freedoms. If I endeavour to clear the obstacles from the path of my own self-fulfilment, without actively considering the well-being of the others (that is, if I am active, without being moral), I am not exercising positive freedom. If I am liberated by someone else's effort, yet in a merely accidental way, not as a result of his intention to do good for me, again, I am not receiving negative freedom (although I am juristically free). There should be an active moral agent on the one or other side of the freedom interaction. So, not all freedoms are either positive or negative. The two conditions of an interaction between an individual and a social partner, and an existence of moral agency, should be available.

It turns out, on analysis, that contrary to Berlin's belief that negative freedom is freedom in the simplest and most straightforward sense, it is the more complex concept of the two. Its philosophical genesis lies in the critique of positive freedom, and its practical possibility rests on the parallel exercise of liberty in its positive sense.

4.2.4 The difference between juristic and negative freedom

Although many political theorists have done so, I believe that it has been a mistake to equate negative freedom with juristic freedom.[55] The distinction that needs to be made is between *the nature* and *the value* of juristic freedom. While by its nature juristic freedom is morally neutral as it is related to the ordinary good rather than to the moral good, once it has been asserted as valuable, it acquires moral significance. Negative freedom is about the political importance of juristic freedom. Berlin's appeal for negative freedom asserts *the significance* of understanding freedom in juristic terms. Speaking of importance and value introduces moral standards. To assert something as valuable means giving a reason why one should pursue it as an end in itself. If something is important we should aspire to it no matter whether this pleases us or not. In other words, asserting a value is at the same time an appeal to people to adopt a moral framework. Thus, while defending the value of negative freedom, political theorists have left behind the moral neutrality which is otherwise intrinsic to juristic freedom. The message delivered by the concept of negative freedom is not that one should always do as one likes, but that it is important to have a society in which individuals, apart from being expected to perform their civic duties, are allowed to pursue their own ends. What the exponents of negative freedom such J. S. Mill and Isaiah Berlin believe, but do not necessarily state clearly, is that in addition to their civic duties, people should be given the space to do as they like. Therefore I disagree with Baldwin's conclusion that the defenders of positive freedom are exponents of 'ethical naturalism', while the defenders of negative freedom are not.[56] Mill's and Berlin's cases for negative freedom are built on ethical grounds.

4.3   Which freedom is more important?

What we have to bear in mind, in discussing positive and negative freedom, is that we are considering not only the nature of the phenomenon of freedom but also a process of evaluation. The debate about which is the true account of freedom aims to establish which freedom is more important. Green and Berlin acknowledge that there are different interpretations of what freedom is, but they argue that one particular interpretation only should acquire central importance both in our moral evaluation and in our political practice. The debate can be resolved by the answer to the question 'Which is the more important sense of freedom?' To put it in Green's words, which freedom 'forms the goal of social effort'?[57]

Green's theory of human agency offers us the philosophical tools to resolve this dilemma. His explanation about why moral freedom is more important than juristic freedom gives us the basis on which we can compare freedoms. Once we have the grounds for comparison, we can extend its application and arrive at conclusions which Green himself fell short of reaching.

Green's argument that moral freedom is more important than juristic freedom is based on the observation that it is the former freedom for which we have a stronger need, that fulfils us better. Moral freedom 'overrules' juristic freedom as once we have the latter we then go on to aspire to the former. Green's argument is underpinned by his belief that the disposition for pursuing a moral good is higher and nobler than the disposition for pursuing ordinary good. I go along with Green here. The very definition of moral good implies a state of overcoming one's habitual self-centred disposition. The element of self-transcendence inherent in moral behaviour gives grounds to the claim that a moral act has a higher status than an ordinary act.

What Green fails to see is that the change of perspective changes the result of the evaluation. There are always two perspectives from which we judge the importance of freedom – the internal and the external. An individual should judge his own and other people's freedom from two standards. Adopting a moral disposition yields different results depending on whose freedom it is we are evaluating. When I take a decision about how I should act, or which kind of freedom I should pursue, I am in a position to believe that a moral action, and accordingly moral freedom, is more important. In my evaluation of my conduct I am justified in ascribing a higher status to the pursuit of moral freedom than to the pursuit of juristic freedom. This is the perspective Green adopts when he argues that moral freedom holds priority over juristic freedom. He pays less attention to the other perspective: the perspective of judging someone else's freedom.

When it comes to deciding for other people, the only good one can do for them is ordinary good. The freedom one can provide for others is a juristic freedom. I can help a fellow human being to do as she likes, but I can never undertake a moral act on her behalf; I cannot fulfil her moral freedom for her. To adopt a moral disposition means to treat others as ends in themselves, that is, to treat them as agents who need ordinary goods, to act on the understanding that like us, they also behave within a self-centred disposition. If

I am to decide what the freedom is that it is my duty to provide for my fellow human beings, I should assume that they are entitled to be free to do as they like. Giving priority to other people's juristic freedom over my juristic freedom is in fact the very essence of exercising moral freedom. In acting morally, I achieve my moral freedom by providing juristic freedom to others – I provide them with more opportunity to do as they like. What is moral liberty to me translates as juristic liberty to others.

By not fully accounting for negative freedom, Green does not register this shift of criteria about the value of freedom. A moral sanction can only be self-imposed. I can say to myself that the most worthy freedom is that of altruistic conduct; I could also commend moral freedom to others. None the less I should respect their freedom to do as they choose. Berlin's defence of negative freedom expresses the belief that a person should not dismiss others' demands for freedom on the grounds that the liberties they are seeking may not be part of moral conduct. A person should be strict with herself and generous to others, and ideally this attitude would be reciprocated. The difference of standards which I commend in judging one's own and other people's freedom is not hypocrisy but awareness of the fact that a moral stance can be adopted only from within a personal perspective. Through the eyes of a moral agent one gives priority to *his moral freedom* over his juristic freedom, and to *others' juristic freedom* over his juristic freedom.

The argument I have developed here is in principle the same as the argument in section 3.4 about the unique position of the self, and in section 2.7 about the value of perfection and the value of the individual. In all these cases I have pursued the consequences of the fact that moral motivation (and the aspiration for perfection) can be only personally adopted. This fact implies that the nature of the same good changes depending on the standpoint of assessment. The same object can be a moral good to the person who provides it and an ordinary good to the person who receives it. Also, the priority of different goods changes depending on whose are the goods that we are evaluating. I value the state of my self-fulfilment higher than the state of myself short of such fulfilment. However, I should value others equally to myself and to each other, independently of how far they have reached in their path of self-improvement. I can judge myself according to my achievements and be unhappy if I am not doing as well as I believe I should, but I have to respect others for what they are.

4.4 Conclusion

This chapter has argued that the division between positive and negative freedom reflects a genuine difference between two types of human action: ordinary and moral. By registering the fact that freedom is used in different senses, and by explaining them through a theory of human agency, Green makes a lasting contribution to the philosophical analysis of freedom. He also applies his theory of the different senses of freedom into political theory by developing the concept of positive freedom on the basis of his notion of moral freedom. This chapter argues that it is important to observe the change that takes place when we move from the theory of the will to the theory of political practice, that is, from discussing the dichotomy between juristic and moral freedom, to the dichotomy between negative and positive freedom. While in the first instance we are addressing a dichotomy between moral neutrality and moral perfection, in the second instance, the distinction is based on the different position of the free agent within the social interactions that constitute freedom. One exercises negative or positive freedom depending on whether one is a recipient or a provider of moral goods. I have gained grounds for this observation by bringing forward Green's theory of the moral conduct and by deriving from it the conclusions that: moral good cannot exist without ordinary good; a moral deed has an agent and a recipient, and for the recipient the delivered good is ordinary good. I have argued that the evaluation of the importance of freedom depends on whose freedom is being evaluated. Only if a person assesses his own freedom can he decide that moral freedom takes priority over juristic freedom. When someone else's freedom has to be decided upon, juristic freedom is to be deemed more important. A person's moral fulfilment goes hand in hand with her respect and concern for other people's ordinary well-being, that is, their juristic freedom.

5
Rights in Green's Political Theory: Universal or Historical?[1]

The theory of rights is presented in Green's *Lectures on the Principles of Political Obligation* (hereafter, *Principles*).[2] Green expresses strong disagreement with the concept of 'natural' rights (defended by Spinoza, Hobbes, Locke and Rousseau)[3] and he also rejects the idea that we have rights as a result of 'consent'. He claims that the 'doctrine that the rights of government are founded on the consent of the governed is a confused way of stating the truth that the institutions by which man is moralised ... express a conception of a common good'.[4] Green argues that we are entitled to rights because this enables us to fulfil our moral agency, and thus, to contribute to the common good. The purpose of rights should not be seen as a protection of the individual from social authorities, because 'a right against society, as such, is an impossibility'.[5] Rights should be exercised for the purpose of creating an ever better community where individuals contribute to the common good and treat each other as equals, on a voluntary basis. The concept of 'natural' rights has developed as a result of the philosophical failure to see that we have rights only as members of a society where the social practice of mutual respect has already taken place.

The main features of Green's theory of rights are his critique of the concept of natural rights and his analysis of the role of society and public institutions in the process of introducing the practice of human rights. This close scrutiny of the social practice of rights leads Green to the conclusion that rights have an historical character. The idea and the language of human rights develop as a result of concrete historical processes. The meaning of rights is to be seen in the context of social interaction.

Having already seen Green's theory of moral agency and the common good as developed in *Prolegomena to Ethics*, it will be very interesting to observe how he deals with the same issues in his *Principles*. However, while in *Prolegomena* the moral personality and the common good were the main issues of analysis, now, in the *Principles*, these issues are employed for the purpose of addressing a range of new topics: human rights, the state, political obligation, property, punishment, war – topics related to political theory. Green is not only going to apply his philosophy to politics, but also continue to develop his ethics in a new theoretical context. While in the *Prolegomena* he argued against Hume and the utilitarians, in the *Principles* he addresses a tradition of political thinkers like Spinoza, Locke, Hobbes, Rousseau and Austin.[6]

In this chapter I shall analyse the philosophical claims made in Green's rights theory and compare them to those made in *Prolegomena*. I will argue that Green's political theory leads him to philosophical conclusions that are slightly different from those reached in his moral philosophy. In *Prolegomena* he argued that all things acquire their meaning in the context of the spiritual principle, the work of which is to be found in the moral nature of the human individual. The concept of rights, however, as developed in *Principles*, fails to take into full account his defence of the human individual, previously portrayed as the sole inspiration of social progress. Furthermore, the assertion of the historical character of human rights may be seen as contradicting the universal character of the spiritual principle displayed in the individual's moral nature.

The argument here is that Green's overall philosophy offers two justifications of human rights. One is explicitly developed in his rights theory and rests on his concept of social recognition. The other is implicitly present in his theory of the human agency and in his moral philosophy. I argue that as presented in his political theory (his theory of rights), Green's justification of rights is not fully satisfactory. Here Green tries simultaneously to resolve two issues: 'What makes the exercise of rights practically possible?' and 'On what grounds are individuals entitled to rights?' Green's preoccupation with the former issue causes him to underestimate the latter. He subordinates the treatment of the issue of the individual's entitlements to rights to the issue of social practice of rights and this, I argue, leads him to philosophical conclusions that contradict his moral philosophy. The latter contains an inspiring argument of the absolute value of the human individual. On the basis of this theory one can 'extract' an argument explaining why human beings are entitled to rights solely on the basis of their need, that is, independently of any social recognition.

Thus Green's overall philosophy poses a dilemma. On what grounds are individuals entitled to rights – on the grounds of need or on the grounds of social recognition? This dilemma concerns the role of the individual in society: should she be seen as the ultimate justification of any effort after social improvement, or as a contributor to a common good? In this chapter I offer a way to reconcile the vision of the individual as someone of absolute value, and the vision of her as a dutiful member of society. I do this by developing the idea that human morality has both a negative and a positive dimension. As human beings, we are negatively moral because we need others to exercise moral behaviour towards us, and we are positively moral because we are able to be agents of such moral behaviour.

This chapter, on the one hand, criticises Green for failing to articulate this dilemma as such and, consequently, for not offering a reconciliation. On the other hand, it brings forward the versatility of Green's overall philosophy by demonstrating that he develops the two perspectives – the universalising and the historical – in his analysis of human rights and thus provides an answer to accusations that his political theory offers only a historical explanation of human rights.[7] The chapter is structured as follows. The first three sections explain Green's rights theory by focusing on the concept of social recognition. I argue that Green speaks of two distinguishable types of social recognition: the practical and the metaphysical. Section 5.4 presents Green's theories of human agency and morality as developed in the *Prolegomena*. It explains how, on the basis of these theories, we can extract a different metaphysical theory of rights. Sections 5.4 and 5.5 offer a reconciliation, respectively, of the two different philosophical justifications of human rights, and of the historical and universalist elements of Green's rights theory.

Although I am somewhat critical of the philosophical conclusions reached in *Principles*, I believe that Green offers a compelling and sound theory of rights. I hope that my representation manages to express, at least in part, its rounded character and its strengths.

5.1   The concept of social recognition

Green's theory of rights rests on his concept of social recognition. Green argues against the idea of natural rights as he does not believe that we can speak about the individual in a meaningful way without taking into account her social environment. He claims that rights exist to the extent that they are recognised by society. This claim has met with many objections. Does it mean that if a society does not recognise any rights, the individual is not entitled to such? Green's defenders point out that his concept of social recognition is a complex one and it accounts not only for the explicit social recognition, but also for implicit forms of agreement.

Tyler,[8] Nicholson,[9] Martin[10] and Thomas[11] have given recent accounts of Green's theory of rights. All of them present a constructive interpretation of this theory by offering an explanation of what might have seemed to other critics, an inconsistency or flaw. 'It is analysis that is needed, however, not impressionistic reaction,' Thomas claims, believing that readers will benefit much more by understanding the full implications of Green's theory of rights, rather than by capitalising on superficial contradictions.[12] None the less, I argue that even a sympathetic account of Green's rights theory will benefit from pointing out the apparent inconsistencies. Whatever explanation we give to Green's rights theory, we have to acknowledge that some tension exists between what he has argued in *Prolegomena* and what he defends in the *Principles*. This tension is recognised by Martin and Thomas. Martin points out that Green bases his definition of rights on two 'principal elements': the idea of the common good and the requirement of social recognition. He notices that 'since either one of these could plausibly be said to exist in the absence of the other, there is a potential tension in Green's theory'.[13] Thomas tries to account for this tension by claiming that Green's 'moral epistemology' diverges from his 'moral ontology'. Thus Thomas acknowledges a necessity for reconciliation, while Tyler, by contrast, does not. Tyler's view, as expressed in reply to Thomas, is that the emphasis on social recognition of rights 'is a necessary aspect of the ontology, not just the epistemology of rights'.[14]

Green's thesis that the existence of human rights is based on social recognition will come as a surprise to anyone who has read and has been persuaded by the *Prolegomena*. If Green was fully consistent with his theory as developed there, he should have argued that rights are based on the specific moral nature of the individual. The justification of rights should come from understanding the metaphysical constitution of human practice. All phenomena can find their ultimate justification in the work of 'the spiritual principle', which is the mechanism of personal experience.

When Green claims that rights are based on social recognition he refers to two related, yet separate, types of social recognition: practical and metaphysical.[15] So through the concept of social recognition Green attempts to give both a practical explanation of the actual process that brings rights into existence *and* a metaphysical justification of rights. I argue that while he is very successful with the former (section 5.2), he is less successful with the latter (section 5.3). The terminology of social recognition, on its own, does not offer a metaphysical justification of rights. The theory explaining better the grounds on which individuals are entitled to rights is to be found elsewhere: in Green's analysis of human agency as developed in the *Prolegomena* (section 5.4).

In addition to speaking of 'social recognition' in both its metaphysical and practical aspects, Green uses the word 'recognition' with two different semantic connotations. The first usage is related to the practical social recognition and bears the meaning of 'agreeing on', 'consenting to'. The second is related to the metaphysical social recognition and describes the process of 'self-overcoming'. This dual usage results from the fact that Green does not speak only of *social* recognition, but also of the individual's recognition. The differences between these will be extensively commented on in section 5.3, in the course of discussing the differences between practical and metaphysical social recognition.

5.2 Practical social recognition

Green's insistence on the importance of social recognition with respect to rights is related to his desire to account for the practical procedure through which rights come into existence. The role of society with respect to the practical implementation of rights looms large. The individual is the agent who acts morally, yet society is 'the agent' who gives rights. It is because Green is predominantly concerned with the question 'How do rights come into existence?' that his definition of rights is so heavily loaded with arguments about social recognition. Green's notion of the practical social recognition of rights is very complex because he wants to imbue it with metaphysical meanings. This notion contains within itself a theory of society, of public consciousness and of the state. I will explain the notion of practical social recognition by following his train of thought. The first stage is the realisation that rights *are given* to the individual by the society. The second is the assessment of the practical implications that follow from that.

Rights are powers which are given to the individual by her fellow human beings. One enjoys rights only so far as these are guaranteed and protected by society. How is that possible? How does society guarantee rights? Or, more precisely, how does society act unanimously? The existence of rights implies a social agreement as to which are the particular powers that should be recognised as rights, and as to the fact that all should act unanimously in guaranteeing these rights. If some recognise my rights but others violate them, I do not have proper rights. In the exercise of my rights, society and I act as partners. I carry the powers which can be exercised as rights, while society recognises them as rights, guarantees and protects them. As 'the others' are my partner, they have to act out of a 'common consciousness' and out of a 'common will'. This is the most difficult step towards introducing rights into practice: having society work as a whole, as a unit; developing a society which unanimously shares the value of the individual's well-being. One of the arguments made by Green is that society will recognise an individual's rights if there is thereby some obvious benefit for society as a whole. There should be some agreeable reason why the individual should have his powers guaranteed. While explaining the grounds on which rights unrecognised by the state should be so recognised, Green claims:

> The assertion by the citizen of any right, however, which the state does not recognise must be founded on a reference to an *acknowledged* social good. ... The reason that an assertion of an illegal right must be founded on reference to *acknowledged* social good is that, as we have seen, no exercise of a power, however

abstractedly desirable for the promotion of human good it might be, can be claimed as a right unless there is some common consciousness of utility shared by the person making the claim and those on whom it is made.[16]

Here Green is arguing that the process of social recognition demands that the individual exercises the powers he claims as rights for the benefit of society. Green advances the idea that rights come about as a result of a long process of social interaction during which 'some consciousness of utility shared' by all is being created. It is only on the basis of this 'public consciousness' that rights can come into practice.[17]

Green makes it very clear that he is speaking about the practical process which leads to the introduction of rights; not about what ought to be the case, but what is the case. He immediately continues to say that '[i]t is not a question whether or not it [the asserted illegal right] ought to be claimed as a right; it simply can *not* be except on this condition'.[18] None the less, he does not view this practical process as unjust or inhumane. He recognises its logic and tries to explain it in terms which make it acceptable.

Green's explanation is as follows. It is true that reality is full of examples of states where abuse of human rights is officially sanctioned, the most obvious case being that of slavery. However, even if the state refuses to recognise rights which we may consider basic, there still exist smaller societies within the state which do recognise these rights. In the case of slavery, there always exists some minimal community of relatives or fellow-slaves amongst whom each slave is treated as a human being. 'The slave thus derives from his social relations a real right which the law of the state refuses to admit.'[19] This small society is the basis on which a social movement for slave rights can rest. The slaves will have their rights properly observed – that is, they will break free from slavery – when this society grows in numbers. Without a minimal society sharing a common consciousness of human respect towards each individual slave, the cause of slave rights is doomed to failure.

Now we can better understand Green's concept of practical social recognition. Green's emphasis is not so much on the 'recognition' but on the formation of a social consciousness. What Green wants to explain to his audience is that without the existence of public consciousness we are as far from rights as we can be. His opponents are those who believe that rights are 'natural', that rights inhere in the individual regardless of their recognition by the rest. To his opponents Green wants to explain that without 'the rest' there are no rights. Green defends the idea of 'recognition' in a very wide sense. Recognition of rights is part of the process that creates public consciousness. The latter can arise only within a practical interactive environment. A better term for Green to express the idea behind his concept of 'social recognition' would have been 'social participation'. The emphasis of Green's protest against natural rights theorists, as well as the weight of his own theory, lies in the fundamental role of 'common consciousness'[20] in the process of enacting human rights: 'We have already seen that a right against society, as such, is an impossibility; that every right is derived from some social relation; that a right against any group of associated men depends on association, as *isos kai homoios* [an equal], with them and with some other men.'[21] We can see that it is not 'social recognition' which is fundamental for the exercise of rights, it is the participation in social relations.

Green's concept of practical social recognition leads us to believe that he defines rights as historical phenomena. A person's idea of what his rights should be must be understandable to his fellow human beings:

> It would have been impossible, e.g., in an ancient state, where the symbol of social union was some local worship, for a monotheistic reformer to claim a right to attempt the subversion of that worship. If a duty to do so had suggested itself, consciousness of the duty could never have expressed itself in the form of a claim of right, in the absence of any possible sense of a public interest in the religious revolution to which the claim could be addressed.[22]

The historical aspect of Green's rights theory is clearly noted by Nicholson. He claims that an 'important corollary of Green's thesis that rights are made by recognition is that no unchanging list of immutable rights can be drawn up, because society develops historically'.[23]

5.3 Metaphysical social recognition

Green uses the term 'social recognition' in a metaphysical sense in so far as 'the others' or 'the society' are part of the metaphysical structure of personal experience. The object in which an individual seeks self-fulfilment has a social character. Her concept of what she is, or of what she should be, is influenced by society. 'No individual can make a consciousness for himself. He always needs a society to make it for him,' Green claims.[24] Furthermore, not only general human experience, but moral experience also, is impossible without the presence of others. The moral character of an action is derived from the personal attitude out of which the action is performed; none the less, the intention of a moral action is always directed towards others. As moral behaviour involves an attempt on behalf of the individual to overcome her self-centred motivation, it aims to satisfy a wider circle of people, not just herself.

Green defines rights by reference to both social recognition *and* a 'moral end'. He views rights as 'powers' which are given to the individual for the purposes of her moral development, that is, to allow her to contribute to a common good. In the many restatements of the definition of rights Green uses various wording to express the same message – that rights are justified by their reference to a moral purpose. Rights are 'powers ... contributory to a common good';[25] they are founded in 'the capacity ... on the part of the individual of conceiving a good as the same for himself and others, and of being determined to action by that conception';[26] '[t]he true conception of "right" depends on ... the individual being what he really is in virtue of a function which he has to fulfil relatively to a certain end, that end being the common well-being of a society'.[27] A major aspect of each of Green's definitions of rights is its underlying moral context.

I claim that the terminology of social recognition represents one of Green's successive attempts to explain the nature of moral action. He argues that the individual develops her moral potential through the act of recognising the rights of her fellow human beings: 'There ought to be rights, because the moral personality – the capacity on the part of the individual for making a common good his own – ought to be developed; and it is developed through rights; i.e. *through the recognition by members of a society of powers in each other* contributory to a common good and the regulation of those powers by that recognition.'[28] The mutual recognition of each other's capacities is part of what morality is about. A moral act is constituted by the individual's determination to contribute to the good of others in the same manner in which he contributes to his own good. Recognising other's rights is a moral act as the agent acts on representation not of his own interest, but of the interest of his fellow human beings. The terminology of social recognition comes as an additional restatement of what constitutes a moral action.

The idea of 'recognising rights', that is, of overcoming a narrowly personal concept of good, is the very idea implied in Green's common good theory. The latter develops the view that one's pursuit of self-fulfilment can be directed towards an object of common benefit. Because moral behaviour implies self-overcoming, it also implies orientation towards others. The intent of a moral act is that the agent is not the sole beneficiary of its results. Overcoming selfishness entails altruism. When Green speaks of rights, he tries to unite his common good theory with his concept of social recognition. The latter is another form of expressing the former.

Unfortunately, Green's attempt to unite his common good theory with the concept of social recognition results in a philosophical error. Green is misled in claiming that the morality of one's action is dependent on *recognition by others*. This is not true, and this is not what Green himself believes to be the case, as I will demonstrate shortly. The moral character of a deed depends on the agent's intention to act in his fellow human beings' interest. Whether his fellow human beings recognise that he has so acted should have no bearing on defining his conduct as moral. It is true that their recognition is important; none the less, it is not *decisive* as to whether his action has been moral. The fact that moral conduct has a social reference does not mean that it rests on social recognition.

Now we can see that Green uses the term 'recognition' in at least two semantically different ways. One of the usages aims to emphasise the importance of social practice (social interaction) for the existence of rights. The other usage is in the sense of 'acting morally'. I recognise your claims for exercising your capacities freely; I treat you as an end; I treat you as an equal – for Green all these statements imply the same meaning: I am acting as a moral agent. The ambiguity in the use of the term 'recognition' comes about because Green shifts indiscriminately between the subjects of recognition. He claims that either society should recognise the individual's right, or that individuals should recognise between themselves their claims on the free exercise of certain powers. The difference is significant. In the first case the subject of recognition is society, in the second, the individual. These cases can be explained by two different theories. To explain how society recognises rights, Green has to explain first how society comes to act as a unit as a result of people living communally and developing common values. To explain the process by which individuals come to recognise the rights of their fellow beings, Green had to analyse the logic of moral behaviour. Clearly, 'recognition' is used in two different senses, one of them as 'registering, seeing, conceding', as I shall now explain, and the second, as 'overcoming one's selfish impulses'.

The function of the practical social recognition, as I have argued in section 5.2, is in the process of forming a unanimous community where people share the same values and treat each other as equals, that is, as subjects of rights. Recognising each other's claims to exercise certain powers ('that spontaneous recognition by each of the claims of all others'[29]) leads to the development of common values. Green refers to the act of recognising as an act of agreeing, consenting, conceding to the same thing. By acknowledging, agreeing on, recognising the same thing as important, we are building a common consciousness:

> There can be no reciprocal claim on the part of a man and an animal each to exercise his powers unimpeded by the other, because there is no consciousness common to them. But a claim founded on such a common consciousness is already a claim *conceded*; already a claim to which reality is given by social recognition, and thus implicitly a right.[30]

Here Green uses 'social recognition' in the sense of agreement reached by interaction; in the sense of interaction out of which common consciousness has emerged. The fact that Green refers to people's recognition as to their ability to understand, is well revealed by the emphasis he places on the dependence of rights on the particular historical context. Any right an individual would claim, however 'desirable in an ideal state of things',[31] has to correspond to an existing public interest; it has to be 'recognisable', 'conceivable' to a minimal circle of people, who will, in turn, guarantee this right.

There arises the question, how much is Green's entire philosophy consistent with his historical interpretation of rights? How does Green reconcile his historical, or practical, account of rights with his metaphysical one? I argue that Green avoids explicit reconciliation, as he uses the term 'recognition' in both a metaphysical and a practical sense. He speaks of a recognition as an act of moral growth, on the one hand, and as an act of agreeing, registering, conceding to, on the other.

My criticism of Green's metaphysical usage of the concept of social recognition is the following. By explaining the nature of moral action through the terminology of social recognition, Green overemphasises the social aspect of human moral nature. The philosophical conclusions that can be drawn on the basis of his rights theory are that the essence of humanity and morality is to be found in the individual's contribution to a social welfare. If, according to Green, one can claim rights only provided that there is some 'utility shared by the person making the claim and those on whom it is made', then one's entitlement to rights rests fully on how useful one can make himself to the others.

5.4   Green's theories of human agency and morality: need as a sufficient justification of rights

What is lacking in the *Principles* and is very clearly present in the *Prolegomena* is Green's emphasis on the inner aspiration towards self-fulfilment. In the latter Green argues that only self-perfection can bring true self-satisfaction. The moral ideal was first defined as the pursuit for perfection (Chapter I, Book III of the *Prolegomena*), and only subsequently (Chapter III, Book III) as the pursuit of the common good. Green dedicates the greater half of Chapter II (Book III) to explaining *'The Personal Character of the Moral Ideal'*.[32] Here the moral ideal is presented as personal in at least two aspects. First in the sense that a person is the home of human spirit:[33]

> [t]he human spirit cannot develop itself according to its idea except in self-conscious subjects. ... The spiritual progress of mankind is thus an unmeaning phrase, unless it means a progress

of personal character and *to* personal character – a progress of which feeling, thinking, and willing subjects are the agents and sustainers, and of which each step is a fuller realisation of the capacities of such subjects.[34]

Secondly, the moral ideal has a personal character in the sense that the individual should be regarded not a means but as the goal of social progress. 'To speak of any progress or improvement or development of a nation or society or mankind, except as relative to some greater worth of persons, is to use words without a meaning.'[35]

How can Green's theory of human agency be related to a theory of human rights? Through very little additional reasoning. According to Green's theory, human nature is such that the individual needs to develop in order to achieve her full potential; she can always be more than what she is now. However, in order to achieve her self-fulfilment, a person needs to exercise and develop her capacities. Now we come to the point discussed in section 2.8. This ever-increasing potential for self-fulfilment goes hand in hand with an ever-increasing vulnerability. As every further self-fulfilment brings more self-satisfaction, the denial of a possibility for self-development causes suffering. If a person is essentially characterised by her permanent potential for improvement, the lack of such improvement undermines her nature as a human being. Moral potential and moral vulnerability are two sides of the same coin.

On the basis of Green's philosophy we can reach the conclusion that human need is a sufficient justification of rights. We are entitled to rights because of the complex character of our needs. Because human nature implies capacity for moral agency, human needs are also moral needs. We should have rights because if we do not have them we cannot realise our humanity. The notions of moral need and moral vulnerability are implicit in both Green's theory of moral agency and in his assertion of the absolute value of the individual.

We can see why, in view of Green's defence of the personal character of the moral ideal, one can find his critique of natural rights puzzling. One would expect that Green would argue that an individual is entitled to rights because of his nature as an agent who permanently pursues a vision of his better self. We have also seen, however, that Green has good reason to criticise the idea of natural rights. He believes that a political theorist should account for the role of society, not only for the formation of rights, but for the formation of human personality. Without that he will end up with a false metaphysical picture of the individual. Green wants to explain that human 'nature' is social. Further to that, Green wants to equate the notion of morality with the social nature of the human individual. He rejects the concept of natural rights because it implies an antagonistic relation between the individual and society. Green concedes that there may be a conflict between the individual and the state, yet not between her and her fellow human beings. He says that rights may be '"natural" in the sense of being independent of, and in conflict with, the laws of the state in which he lives, but they are not independent of social relations'.[36]

However, in his political theory, Green goes too far along the road of asserting the link between the individual's self-fulfilment and her involvement in societal life. In essence, he identifies the individual with her social role. He is justified in arguing that an antagonism between the individual and society should not be assumed, yet he is wrong in ruling it out as a possibility. Such antagonism is possible when someone is uprooted from his own environment and forced to live in exile, among people of whose society he has not been a member. There are other possible scenarios where a person may find herself 'detached' from her immediate surrounding. Typical is Green's own example of the social reformer, whose 'very essence ... consists in his being the corrector and not the exponent of the common feeling of his day'.[37] What is it, according to Green, that gives the social reformer the confidence that he is pursuing the right cause, regardless of any lack of public support? 'The breath of his life,' Green claims, 'is inspired from above, not drawn up from below. Those flashes of religious enlightenment which from time to time break on the slumbers of mankind often resemble in their history the discovery of scientific truth.'[38] The insight carried by the social reformer is how we, in the particular circumstances in which we live, as a society can lead a good life. And explaining what a good life is is one of Green's philosophical achievements in *Prolegomena*. The absolute good for Green is human perfection: 'the object generally sought as good [must be] a state of mind or character of which the attainment, or approach to attainment, by each is itself a contribution to its attainment by every one else.'[39] There he also claims that 'it is only so far as this development and direction of personality [to contribute to human perfection] is obtained for all who are capable of it (as presumably everyone who says "I" is capable), that human society, either in its widest comprehension or in any of its particular groups, can be held to fulfil its function, to realise its idea as it is in God.'[40]

Although Green believes that human rights have an historical character, he does not doubt for a moment that our moral agency is 'ahistorical'. There was no stage of humanity preceding that whereby human beings were capable of regarding their fellow human beings' good as equal to their own. The capacity to endorse other people's good as part of one's own idea of good is the very essence of humanity: 'We may take it, then, as an ultimate fact of human history – a fact without which there would not be such a history, and which is not in turn deducible from any other history – that out of sympathies of animal origin, through their presence in a self-conscious soul, there arise interests as of a person in persons.'[41] The human ability to pursue self-fulfilment in a self-conscious and 'self-distancing' way is ahistorical. The very content of a moral ideal may develop throughout human history,[42] but not the fact that human beings have the capacity to further their own well-being by pursuing moral ideals.

5.5   Rights as an expression of negative freedom: negative and positive morality

The philosophical grounds of human rights are to be found in the moral nature of the human agent, but it is in how to define this moral nature that Green remains ambiguous. Green does say that '[t]here ought to be rights, because the moral personality – the capacity on the part of an individual for making a common good his own – ought to be developed; and it is developed through rights'.[43] However, Green is ambiguous as to why moral personality should be developed. His rights theory leaves us with the impression that people ought to be moral because, by being moral, they contribute to the common well-being. Yet Green also implies that the reason for helping someone to become a moral agent is that this is part and parcel of developing his personality in general, of his achieving self-fulfilment and leading a full life. The ambiguity is the following: does morality consist in doing good for the others, and therefore, rest on social recognition, or does it consist in the pursuit for self-improvement and the demand to receive moral treatment? Although these two aspects of the nature of morality are related, when it comes to the issue of human rights, they do represent two different grounds for justifying rights.

Green gives us a clue as how to resolve this ambiguity. He claims that human rights are about 'the negative realisation' of one's powers. The way Green uses the terminology of positive and negative freedom suggests to me the possibility of speaking respectively of positive and negative morality. In a statement which I shall quote shortly, Green speaks, in essence, about negative freedom. This statement is easily overlooked because he does not develop it further, and because he is generally thought of as the exponent of positive freedom. Green writes:

> Rights are what may be called the negative realisation of this power [the power of the individual freely to make the common good his own]. That is, they realise it in the sense of providing for its free exercise, of securing the treatment of one man by another as equally free with himself, but they do not realise it positively, because their possession does not imply that in any active way the individual makes a common good his own. The possession of them, however, is the condition of this positive realisation of the moral capacity. ...[44]

This statement casts light on how Green uses the terminology of 'negative' and 'positive' exercise of freedom. In Chapter 4 we saw that the individual has negative freedom as a recipient of moral treatment, and positive freedom as an active moral agent. Rights can be seen as a negative exercise of power in the sense that the individual does what she does, thanks to the help of others; she uses her freedom as guaranteed to her, as given to her by the rest.

Green's use of 'negative'/'positive' terminology in explaining the exercise of powers, as well as his practical and moral philosophy from *Prolegomena*, have led me to the observation that human morality is characterised not only by the goods one can actively produce, but also by what one needs (section 2.8). This terminology suggests a constructive way to describe better individual moral nature. We can speak of *positive and negative human morality* in order to account simultaneously for the fact that one may act in a self-disinterested way, on the one hand, and that one needs to be a recipient of self-disinterested action, on the other. Once we spell out fully the negative aspect of morality, we have clear grounds for the justification of rights: we are entitled to rights because we are negatively moral. As opposed to Green, whose concept of social recognition leads to the conclusion that rights are justified through positive morality, I claim that the metaphysical grounds of rights are to be found in negative morality.

5.6   Rights – universal or historical?

As I have repeatedly stated, in his rights theory Green is predominantly occupied in explaining the implications of the actual social practice of rights, not their justification. His account of rights as historical is more explicit than his account of rights as universal. The reconciliation and integration of the two accounts, which we can 'extract' from Green's overall philosophy, is that human entitlement to rights is universal, while substantive definition of human rights is historical. Everyone is entitled to be a recipient of moral attitudes, to be treated as an end, to be regarded as equal by the rest. Rights are universal, as is the moral nature of the human agent. However, concrete substantive rights have an historical character in the sense that they are related to the existing 'social consciousness'. Rights, whether enforced by state legislation or practised by customary law, are always related to social practice. Green's preoccupation with the practical aspect of rights has to be seen as something positive. He thereby advances the theory of rights from the stage where philosophers asserted 'natural rights' on the grounds of a profound understanding of human nature. Green's theory leads to the conclusion that it is more important to assess existing possibilities for social improvements than to stick dogmatically to an abstract concept of rights. The theory of universal entitlement to rights should serve as a general orientation as to the purpose of social improvement; but, what is equally important, is finding out and expanding the existing practices of recognising rights. In a sense, it is wrong to enforce a progressive vision of rights in a society which cannot maintain it.[45]

5.7   Conclusion: reconciling the two lines of thought in Green's philosophy

In his overall philosophy Green analyses human practice from two separate perspectives, thus asserting two different conclusions. One of these perspectives, as developed in Green's political theory, and specifically, in his rights theory, focuses on the process of social interaction and draws conclusions about the fundamentally social nature of human experience. The other perspective, as developed in Green's moral philosophy, focuses on the work of the spiritual principle that is always enacted in the individual's personal experience. There Green argues against the idea of any 'impersonal Humanity' and that all things acquire their meaning and value only within a personal context.[46] If we are to give a final account of Green's theory of rights we have to deal with this dilemma: does Green believe that rights have an historical character (that is, they are metaphysically dependent on what the public consciousness is prepared to recognise), or does he have a concept of human individuality which justifies rights in a universal way (that is, we are moral by nature and thus are unconditionally entitled to rights)? As we have seen, this dilemma can be further expressed by a question about what constitutes human moral nature. Where does our moral nature reside: in our altruistic action expressed in active involvement in societal life, or in our personal sensitivity as human beings who are in a constant process of self-development and thus in constant need of exercising our personal capacities? I have argued that although in his political philosophy Green has committed himself to the former option, in his moral philosophy he has engaged himself with the latter.

The terminology of positive and negative morality which I have introduced reconciles two fundamental aspects of human nature: its fundamentally personal, and its fundamentally social, character. Our capacity for moral action and our need for moral treatment are two sides of the same coin. Delivering the message about the intrinsic social dimension of human individuality – Green's concern – should not be at the cost of abandoning his theory of the personal embeddedness of the spiritual principle. It is true that our fulfilment always necessitates social context, yet it is always *a* human agent who is being fulfilled, and thus her fulfilment always bears her particular personal mark. The moral nature of the human character is not exhibited solely in the active commitment to others' good, but also in the need for moral action on behalf of the others.

Spelling out the fact that moral nature has a negative and a positive side bears important political implications in so far as there are always two possibilities as to how these two sides will cohabit. It is possible that they can exist in harmony, that is, that a person consumes moral resources but she also provides such for the others in return. However, there exists the possibility of a conflict where she needs moral treatment but does not necessarily offer such herself. A political theorist needs to be able to offer solutions, should this conflict occur. Green's theory of human rights does not address the problem in a straightforward manner, but his philosophy provides resources for resolving the question: 'Is one entitled to rights when the public consciousness of one's fellow human beings does not recognise such rights?'

Conclusion

Conclusion

Tracing the phenomenological elements in Green's philosophy has brought to light aspects that have not been addressed before. I have analysed in turn Green's theories of human practice, moral action, common good, freedom and rights, and all these analyses have consistently led to one observation: Green employs two different perspectives in all of his philosophical enquiries and has, therefore, presented us with fundamental philosophical dilemmas. What is of higher priority: human perfection or human well-being in general, independently of how 'well-being' is understood? What is the essence of morality: the need to make the best of ourselves and do as much good for others as we can or the need to be accepted by others the way we are (ordinary and imperfect)? Which is the more important freedom: the freedom to pursue your own vision of the good, or the freedom that is associated with the fulfilment of your duties? How do we justify rights: on the basis of human need or on the basis of social recognition? As mentioned earlier, Green's philosophy has led us to these dilemmas because he has always explored two perspectives that have not been easy to reconcile. Green has defined human practice as guided simultaneously by a 'self-seeking' principle and a 'self-distinguishing' principle (Chapter 1); he has defined morality as an adoption of a self-disinterested disposition, but he has also defined it as the pursuit of the unconditional good (Chapter 2); he has introduced two senses of the common good – one in the sense of moral good, one in the sense of ordinary good (Chapter 3); he has introduced two concepts of freedom, juristic and true, claiming that true freedom is more important, yet believing that juristic freedom is indispensable (Chapter 4); he argued that we have rights only to the extent that we live in a society, yet he believed that there is social prosperity only to the extent that there is personal self-fulfilment (Chapter 5). I have criticised Green for not having resolved these dilemmas but I have viewed the fact that his philosophy has brought them forward, as a major advantage. The fact that Green has explored different perspectives reveals the versatility and the depth of his philosophical insights. The dilemmas Green has led us to cannot be fully resolved. The only available resolution is the awareness that in assessing the moral qualities of a particular conduct we have two different perspectives which, at least on some level, preclude each other; the awareness that the change of perspective brings along change in priorities (for example, between true and juristic freedoms) or change in the moral evaluation (for example, whether the common good represents moral or ordinary good).

Green's understanding of human practice as a dynamic process of self-objectification and his understanding of moral action as a process of adopting a self-disinterested disposition reflect the phenomenological character of his overall philosophy. His theories of morality and the common good explain how the change of an agent's inner disposition results in a change of the nature of her action. A personal transformation produces a transformation in the value of the objects pursued by the person. The same thing done with a different motivation carries a different moral value. We can see why Green, as a philosopher who does phenomenological research, has developed philosophy where 'perspectives' have grown to be major components.

Notes

Introduction

1 Kant claims that 'the understanding is itself the legislature facing nature, that is to say without understanding there would not be a nature at all'. *Critique of Pure Reason*, ed. by Vasilis Politis (London: Everyman, 1993) p. 136.

2 Melvin Richter, *The Politics of Conscience: T. H. Green and his Age* (London: Weidenfeld and Nicolson, 1964).

3 In his article 'Self-love and Altruism' (*Social Philosophy and Policy* 14:1 [1997] 122–57), David Brink refers to Green's philosophy in support of his concept of 'metaphysical egoism'. For Thomas Hurka, Green is one of the classical exponents of the theory of perfectionism – a theory that Hurka himself embraces. See his *Perfectionism* (Oxford: Oxford University Press, 1993).

4 In this text I alternate between the use of female and male pronouns.

5 Edmund Husserl, *The Crisis of European Sciences and Transcendental Phenomenology*, trans. by David Carr (Evanston, IU.: Northwestern University Press, 1970). Hereafter, *The Crisis*.

6 T. H. Green, *Prolegomena to Ethics* (Oxford: Clarendon Press, 1890). Hereafter *Prolegomena*. In quotations, the first number shows the page number, the second, the section number (for example, *Prolegomena*, 36, 38).

7 See Paul Harris and John Morrow's notes in their edition of Green's *Lectures on the Principles of Political Obligation and Other Writings* (Cambridge: Cambridge University Press, 1986) p. 354.

8 *Prolegomena*, 1, 1.

9 *Prolegomena*, 1, 1. For the generally uncertain status of the discipline of moral philosophy, see 'The Province of Ethics', in *Collected Works of T. H. Green, Volume 5*, ed. by Peter Nicholson (Bristol: Thoemmes Press, 1997) pp. 193–4.

10 *Prolegomena*, 3, 2.

11 *Prolegomena*, 2, 1.

12 *Prolegomena*, 2, 1.

13 *Prolegomena*, 4, 2.

14 *Prolegomena*, 7, 5.

15 *Prolegomena*, 4, 2.

16 *Prolegomena*, 6, 5.

17 *Prolegomena*, 6–7, 5.

18 *Prolegomena*, 7, 5.

19 *Prolegomena*, 7, 5.

20 *Prolegomena*, 9, 6.

21 *Prolegomena*, 9, 7.

22 Husserl started to write *The Crisis of European Sciences and Transcendental Phenomenology* in 1935 (Part I and Part II of the book are based on a series of lectures he delivered in Prague in November 1935), but did not finish it because he was terminally ill. He himself acknowledged that it was the best expression of his ideas. Alfred Schutz has reported that 'in the last conversation which the writer had the good fortune of having with Husserl, he repeatedly designated this series of essays as the summary and the crowning achievement of his life work'. Alfred Schutz, 'Phenomenology and the Social Sciences', in *Philosophical Essays in Memory of Edmund Husserl*, ed. Marvin Farber (Cambridge, Mass.: Harvard University Press, 1940) p. 165. The quote is from David Carr in his translator's introduction to *The Crisis*, p. xxix.

23 *The Crisis*, pp. 3–4.

24 *The Crisis*, p. 5.

25 The Vienna lecture was presented to the Vienna Cultural Society on 7 and 10 May 1935. It appeared in the German edition of *The Crisis* as the third 'Abhandlung', pp. 314–48. In Carr's translation of *The Crisis*, the Vienna lecture is given as Appendix I, pp. 269–99. The quotes from the Vienna lecture will be referred to *The Crisis*. *The Crisis*, p. 270.

26 *The Crisis*, p. 8.

27 *The Crisis*, p. 6.

28 *The Crisis*, p. 6.

29 *The Crisis*, p. 9.

30 Husserl develops the concept of Europe as a cultural formation more extensively in the Vienna lecture. There he argues that there is something that binds the nations of Europe together to the extent that Europe becomes the name of a cultural phenomenon, not simply of a geographical area: 'the title "Europe" clearly refers to the unity of a spiritual life, activity, creation, with all its ends, interests, cares, and endeavours, ... institutions, organizations' (*The Crisis*, p. 273). In this spiritual sense, the United States and the English Dominions, Husserl claims, belong to Europe. Husserl explains the emergence of the European phenomenon by reference to two events which took place during the Renaissance: the revival of interest in ancient Greek philosophy and the emergence of the mathematised natural sciences. The idea that rational knowledge must guide human life was central to both.

31 *The Crisis*, p. 12, emphasis added. Only *'Existenz'* is italicised by Husserl.

32 The Vienna lecture was originally entitled 'Philosophy in the Crisis of European Mankind'. In November 1935, six months after giving this lecture in Vienna, Husserl gave a series of lectures in Prague which became the basis of *The Crisis*. The series of lectures was entitled 'The Crisis of European Sciences and Psychology'.

33 *The Crisis*, p. 22.

34 *The Crisis*, p. 46.

35 *The Crisis*, p. 44.

36 *The Crisis*, p. 47.

37 *The Crisis*, p. 50.
38 *The Crisis*, p. 52.
39 *The Crisis*, p. 50.
40 *The Crisis*, p. 52.
41 *The Crisis*, p. 111.
42 *The Crisis*, pp. 52–3.
43 *The Crisis*, p. 60.
44 *The Crisis*, p. 68.
45 *The Crisis*, p. 67.
46 *The Crisis*, p. 69.
47 I have based my analysis of the phenomenological reduction on Husserl's *Cartesian Meditations*, trans. by Dorion Cairns (The Hague: Martinus Nijhoff, 1960) (hereafter, *Meditations*), and on *The Crisis*.
48 *Meditations*, p. 17, emphasis added.
49 *Meditations*, pp. 19–20.
50 In his *Cartesian Meditations*, as indicated by the title, Husserl explains phenomenological reduction by comparing it to Cartesian doubt. Descartes' doubt is not sceptical, but methodological: he does not doubt the ultimate possibility of rational truth, as Hume does, for example, but only those aspects of human experience that are not presented to us with absolute certainty. Thus Husserl develops his idea of the *epochē* by analysing and interpreting Descartes' train of thought in *Meditations on the First Philosophy* (See René Descartes, *Key Philosophical Writings*, trans. Elizabeth S. Haldane and G. R. T. Ross, Wordsworth Editions, Ware, Hertfordshire, 1997).
51 *Meditations*, pp. 20–1.
52 *Meditations*, p. 21.
53 Husserl believes that conceiving of things as entities in themselves is a cultural phenomenon that derives from science. Scientific objectivism has produced an attitude of general objectivism. For Husserl the necessity of bracketing the existence of the world is related to his belief that the validity of science itself should be suspended. As a result of science, the world has become a place of objectivistic attitudes. I believe that Husserl's analysis of the nature of science applies to human nature in general. The tendency to 'objectify' and to seek certainty is a characteristic of human practice. That is why this tendency cannot necessarily be qualified as 'wrong'. (See Maria Dimova, 'T. H. Green as a Phenomenologist: Linking British Idealism and Continental Phenomenology', *Angelaki: Journal of the Theoretical Humanities* 3:1 [1998] 77–88.) However, as many of the misconceptions of human knowledge are underpinned by this aspect of human nature, articulating it is of great importance.
54 Husserl speaks about transcendental phenomenology and transcendental ego; he calls his phenomenological reduction also 'transcendental reduction'.
55 I say 'suggests' as Husserl himself adheres to dichotomies such as that between the psychological and the transcendental ego. We shall see that Green's attitude to such dichotomies is more dialectical. In his discussion

of the different senses of freedom (addressed in Chapter 4), Green criticises Kant for speaking about two egos or two selves. Green accepts the
distinction between the 'pure ego' and the 'empirical ego', but only to the
extent that it represents two stages of human development. He insists,
however, that this is one and the same 'self', and not two different selves.
See section 4.1.2 below.

56 *Meditations*, p. 13.

57 Andrew Vincent's comments have helped me to articulate the connection
between Husserl's phenomenological reduction and Green's moral theory.

58 *The Crisis*, p. 137.

59 *The Crisis*, p. 235.

Chapter 1

1 I am grateful to the comments of Peter Nicholson, Giuseppe Tassone and
Colin Tyler.

2 T. H. Green, 'Review of J. Watson: "Kant and his English Critics"', *Works
of Thomas Hill Green, Volume III*, ed. by R. L. Nettleship (London:
Longmans, Green, and Co, 1889) p. 148. Hereafter *Works III*.

3 See *Prolegomena*, Book III, Chapter III, subheading A 'Reason as Source of
the Idea of a Common Good'.

4 See *Prolegomena*, Book II, Chapter II, 'Desire, Intellect, and Will'.

5 'Transcendental' as referring to the conditions which make experience
possible is different from 'transcendent' as referring to what lies beyond
experience. My reference to transcendentalism relies heavily on its distinct meaning of reference to the preconditions of experience.

6 Immanuel Kant, *Critique of Pure Reason*, translation based on Meiklejohn,
ed. by Vasilis Politis (London, Vermont: Everyman, 1996) p. 44.

7 *Ibid.*, p. 43.

8 *Ibid.*, p. 30.

9 *Ibid.*, p. 42.

10 *Ibid.*, p. 165.

11 *Ibid.*, p. 45.

12 *Ibid.*, p. 32.

13 Ernst Cassirer, *An Essay on Man* (New Haven, Conn.: Yale University
Press, 1972) p. 60. See also Cassirer, *The Philosophy of Symbolic Forms*,
trans. Ralph Manheim, 3 vols. (New Haven, Conn.: Yale University Press,
1953–57) vol. I, p. 80.

14 *Ibid.*, p. 60.

15 Edmund Husserl, *The Crisis of European Sciences and Transcendental
Phenomenology*, trans. David Carr (Evanston, Ill.: Northwestern University
Press, 1970) p. 97, p. 69.

16 Often the terms 'transcendent' and 'transcendental' are used synonymously,
both meaning things that transcend sense-experience (see Anthony
Quinton's entry 'Transcendentalism', in *The Oxford Companion to Philosophy*,
ed. by Ted Honderich [Oxford: Oxford University Press, 1995] pp. 878–9).

17 *Prolegomena*, 15, 11. The first number shows the number of the page, the second, the number of the section.

18 *Prolegomena*, 39, 37.

19 *Prolegomena*, 38, 36.

20 *Prolegomena*, 53, 51.

21 The contradiction in Green's position with respect to the independent existence of the non-human world had been noted by many critics, most famously by Andrew Seth (*Hegelianism and Personality* [Edinburgh & London: William Blackwood, 1887]). Most recently, however, it has been summed up by Tyler: 'Green vacillates constantly between treating the external world (and therefore unperceived sensations) on the one hand, as "blank nothing" and, on the other, as the source of our perceived sensations' (*Thomas Hill Green (1836–1882) and the Philosophical Foundations of Politics* [Lewiston: The Edwin Mellen Press, 1997] p. 16).

22 Tyler, *Thomas Hill Green (1836–1882) and the Philosophical Foundations of Politics*, p. 33.

23 *Prolegomena*, 53, 51.

24 Anthony Quinton, 'T. H. Green's "Metaphysics of Knowledge"', paper given at the conference 'Anglo-American Idealism 1865–1927', Oxford, July 1997.

25 Green, *Works of Thomas Hill Green, Volume I*, ed. by Nettleship, (London: Longman, Green, and Co, 1894) p. 149. Hereafter *Works I*.

26 John Skorupski, *English-Language Philosophy 1750–1945* (Oxford: Oxford University Press, 1993) p. 85.

27 *Prolegomena*, 53, 51; 47, 45.

28 *Prolegomena*, 39, 37.

29 See *Prolegomena*, section 51.

30 Peter Hylton, 'The Metaphysics of T. H. Green', *History of Philosophy Quarterly*, 2:1 (1985) 91–110.

31 These two introductions were published also in *Works I*, under the title: Introductions to Hume's 'Treatise of Human Nature': I General Introduction, pp. 1–299; II Introduction to the Moral Part of Hume's 'Treatise', pp. 300–71. More of Green's views on Hume's philosophy and its impact on the dominant philosophical tendencies of his time are to be found in 'Popular Philosophy in its Relation to Life', *Works III*, pp. 92–125.

32 Hylton, 'The Metaphysics of T. H. Green', p. 91.

33 W. H. Walsh, 'Green's Criticism of Hume', *The Philosophy of T. H. Green*, ed. by Andrew Vincent (Aldershot: Gower, 1986) 21–35, p. 31.

34 Norman Kemp Smith argues that Green misinterpreted Hume's philosophy as he failed to define properly Hume's intentions and task. See his *The Philosophy of David Hume* (London: Macmillan – now Palgrave, 1960) Chapter IV, 79–105; and Walsh 'Green's Criticism of Hume', p. 32.

35 David Hume, *A Treatise of Human Nature*, ed. by L. A. Selby-Bigge (Oxford: Clarendon Press, 1888). Hereafter *Treatise*.

36 Husserl, *The Crises of European Sciences*, p. 69, note 1. In the second half of his philosophical career Husserl esteemed very highly the contribution of

the British empiricists, and Hume in particular, to the emergence of the phenomenological idea. 'Often he gave them credit for having developed the first though inadequate type of phenomenology.' H. Spiegelberg, *The Phenomenological Movement* (The Hague: Martinus Nijhoff, 1982) p. 85.

37 *Treatise*, p. 273.

38 See *Treatise*, p. 266.

39 *Treatise*, p. 270.

40 Hume is prepared to acknowledge and even analyse the existence of 'high-ranking' feelings such as a 'sense of duty', 'the sense of justice and injustice', 'moral sentiments' and 'moral taste', but fervently denies reason any participation in their constitution. Sometimes he uses the term 'sentiment' in the meaning of 'thought', or 'consideration': '... [I] shall here continue to open up a little more distinctly my sentiments on that subject' (*Treatise*, p. 527).

41 Green acknowledges as an achievement the fact that Hume presents the sphere of morals as 'artificial', as a 'product' of man. In 'Popular Philosophy in its Relation to Life' he writes: 'in seeking to know the moral world, man is dealing with a world which he has made for himself. No one asserts this more strongly than Hume, when he is maintaining the 'artificial' character of the most essential social virtues.' *Works III*, p. 112.

42 *Treatise*, p. 463.

43 *Treatise*, p. 464.

44 Hume's critique of reason is similar to Husserl's critique of scientific objectivism.

45 *Treatise*, p. 464.

46 *Treatise*, p. 458.

47 *Treatise*, p. 468.

48 *Treatise*, p. 458.

49 *Works III*, p. 115.

50 *Works III*, p. 118.

51 See 'Popular Philosophy in its Relation to Life', *Works III*, 109–11.

52 *Prolegomena*, 92, 86.

53 *Prolegomena*, 160, 154.

54 *Prolegomena*, 96, 92.

55 *Prolegomena*, 104, 100.

56 *Prolegomena*, 92, 86.

57 Joy Pople, 'Jacob and Esau; Genesis 25:19–26:5', Internet, 1998.

58 *Ibid.*

59 'Esau ate, drank, got up and went away. He did not care about the birthright. He did not think about the future; he just thought how to get what he wanted now.' *Ibid.*

60 *Prolegomena*, 100, 96.

61 This is a reference to Hume.

62 *Prolegomena*, 104, 100.

63 *Prolegomena*, 104, 100.

64 *Prolegomena*, 93–4, 88.

65 *Prolegomena*, 104, 100.
66 In the *Prolegomena* 'Desire' and 'Understanding' are with capital letters.
67 *Prolegomena*, 135, 130, emphasis added.
68 *Prolegomena*, 136, 131.
69 *Prolegomena*, 137, 132.
70 *Prolegomena*, 123, 118.
71 See *Prolegomena*, 210: Subheading A of Chapter III, Book III.
72 *Prolegomena*, Book II, Chapter II 'Desire, Intellect, and Will'.
73 See section 1.2.
74 *Prolegomena*, 155, 150.
75 *Prolegomena*, 54, 51.
76 Tyler, *Thomas Hill Green (1836–1882) and the Philosophical Foundations of Politics*, Chapter Two, sections 4, 5, 6.
77 *Ibid.*, p. 56.
78 *Ibid.*, p. 65.
79 *Ibid.*, p. 56.
80 Henry Sidgwick, *Lectures on the Ethics of T. H. Green, Mr. Herbert Spencer, and J Martineau* (London: Macmillan, 1902) pp. 15–22.
81 Tyler quotes from 'On the Different Senses of "Freedom" as Applied to Will and the Moral Progress of Man' (*Works II*, pp. 308–33), however, the same message is clearly expressed in *Prolegomena*, Book II.
82 Tyler, *Thomas Hill Green (1836–1882) and the Philosophical Foundations of Politics*, p. 67. The quote is from Bernard Bosanquet, *The Principle of Individuality and Value* (London: Macmillan, 1927) p. 333.
83 Avital Simhony also criticises Tyler's interpretation of 'Green's spiritual determinism'. See her review article 'Colin Tyler, *Thomas Hill Green (1836–1882) and the Philosophical Foundations of Politics*', *Bradley Studies* 5:1 (1999) 87–106.

Chapter 2

1 Geoffrey Thomas, *The Moral Philosophy of T. H. Green* (Oxford: Clarendon Press, 1987) p. 72.
2 David Weinstein, 'Between Kantianism and Consequentialism in T. H. Green's Moral Philosophy', *Political Studies*, 41 (1993) 618–35, p. 635.
3 Avital Simhony, 'Was T. H. Green a Utilitarian?', *Utilitas*, 7:1 (1995) 121–44, p. 126.
4 *Prolegomena*, 204, 194.
5 *Prolegomena*, 203, 193.
6 *Prolegomena*, 205, 194.
7 *Prolegomena*, 161, 155.
8 See *Prolegomena*, section 156.
9 *Prolegomena*, 178, 171.
10 *Prolegomena*, 160, 154.
11 *Prolegomena*, 160, 154.
12 *Prolegomena*, 161, 154.

13 Green claims: 'A man may seek to satisfy himself with pleasure, but the pleasure of self-satisfaction can never be that with which he seeks to satisfy himself' (*Prolegomena*, 167, 160).
14 *Prolegomena*, 169, 162.
15 *Prolegomena*, 161, 154.
16 T. L. S. Sprigge, 'Utilitarianism and Idealism: A Rapprochement', *Philosophy* 60 (1985) 447–63, p. 447.
17 *Prolegomena*, 163, 156.
18 *Prolegomena*, 203, 193, emphasis added.
19 *Prolegomena*, 203–4, 193.
20 See *Prolegomena*, section 156.
21 John Stuart Mill, *Utilitarianism*, in *On Liberty and Other Essays*, ed. by John Gray (Oxford: Oxford University Press, 1991) p. 138. Hereafter *Utilitarianism*.
22 *Prolegomena*, 170, 163.
23 *Utilitarianism*, p. 140.
24 *Prolegomena*, 164, 157.
25 *Prolegomena*, 181, 173.
26 *Prolegomena*, 179, 171.
27 *Prolegomena*, 181, 173.
28 *Prolegomena*, 197, 187.
29 *Prolegomena*, 181, 173; 181, 174.
30 *Prolegomena*, 160, 154.
31 *Prolegomena*, 182, 175.
32 *Prolegomena*, 181, 174.
33 *Prolegomena*, 198–9, 189.
34 *Prolegomena*, 199, 189.
35 *Prolegomena*, 276, 257.
36 *Prolegomena*, 273, 253.
37 *Prolegomena*, 204, 194.
38 *Prolegomena*, 204, 194.
39 *Prolegomena*, 203, 193.
40 *Prolegomena*, 180, 172.
41 *Prolegomena*, 203, 193; 204, 194.
42 *Prolegomena*, 204, 194.
43 *Prolegomena*, 205, 194.
44 *Prolegomena*, 205, 194.
45 *Prolegomena*, 257, 240.
46 Colin Tyler, *Thomas Hill Green (1836–1882) and the Philosophical Foundations of Politics* (Lewiston: The Edwin Mellen Press, 1997) pp. 80–2.
47 Weinstein, 'Between Kantianism and Consequentialism in T. H. Green's Moral Philosophy', pp. 634–5.
48 Simhony, 'Was T. H. Green a Utilitarian?'.
49 *Ibid.*, p. 144.
50 *Ibid.*, p. 127.
51 *Ibid.*, p. 126.
52 *Prolegomena*, 193, 184.
53 Section A from Chapter II, Book III of the *Prolegomena*.

54 *Prolegomena*, 189, 180.
55 *Prolegomena*, 191, 182.
56 *Prolegomena*, 193, 184.
57 *Prolegomena*, 194, 184.
58 *Prolegomena*, 193, 184.
59 *Prolegomena*, 196, 186.
60 Thomas Hurka, *Perfectionism* (Oxford: Oxford University Press, 1993) p. 147.
61 *Ibid.*, p. 5.
62 *Ibid.*

Chapter 3

1 Some of the material of this chapter has been already published in Maria Dimova-Cookson, 'T. H. Green's Theory of the Common Good', *Collingwood Studies* vol. VI (1999) 85–109.
2 See Colin Tyler, *T. H. Green (1836–1882) and the Philosophical Foundations of Politics*, (Lewiston: The Edwin Mellen Press, 1997) pp. 96–137; Geoffrey Thomas, *The Moral Philosophy of T. H. Green* (Oxford: Clarendon Press, 1987) p. 254; Andrew Vincent, *The Philosophy of T. H. Green* (Aldershot: Gower, 1986) p. 13.
3 Vincent, *The Philosophy of T. H. Green*, p. 13.
4 *Ibid.*
5 Thomas, *The Moral Philosophy of T. H. Green*, p. 254.
6 *Ibid.*, p. 255.
7 *Prolegomena*, 210, 199.
8 *Ibid.*
9 *Ibid.*
10 Green uses the terms 'social interest' or 'distinctive social interest' (*Prolegomena*, 211, 200).
11 *Prolegomena*, 210, 199.
12 See *Prolegomena*, sections 221–8.
13 *Prolegomena*, 246, 230.
14 *Prolegomena*, 245–6, 229.
15 *Prolegomena*, 247, 231.
16 See *Prolegomena*, sections 229–32.
17 *Prolegomena*, 247, 231.
18 *Prolegomena*, 242, 228.
19 *Prolegomena*, 248, 232.
20 Alan Milne, 'The Common Good and Rights in T. H. Green's Ethical and Political Theory', in *The Philosophy of T. H. Green*, ed. by Andrew Vincent (Aldershot: Gower, 1986) 62–75, p. 69.
21 *Prolegomena*, 249, 232.
22 See Book II ('The Will') of *Prolegomena*.
23 In this context, I would like to mention that David Brink ('Self-Love and Altruism', *Social Philosophy & Policy*, 14:1 [1997] 122–57) addresses Green's salvation argument as a major theoretical resource to his own

concept of 'metaphysical egoism'. He believes this concept resolves the shortcomings of the 'strategical egoism' theory which 'can justify other-regarding duties only towards partners in systems of mutual advantage' (p. 123). The conception of metaphysical egoism 'should lead us to see people's interests as metaphysically, and not just strategically interdependent'. Brink acknowledges the legacy of two traditions: Plato's discussion of love in the *Symposium* and the *Phaedrus* and Aristotle's discussion of friendship and political community in the *Nicomachean Ethics* and the *Politics*, and of Green's discussion of self-realisation and extension of common good in the *Prolegomena to Ethics*. These two traditions offer the insights which help Brink to develop his theory of *'interpersonal psychological continuity'*, and to explain his idea that 'the separateness or diversity of persons is not so fundamental' (pp. 141–2).

24 Milne, 'The Common Good and Rights in T. H. Green's Ethical and Political Theory', p. 69, Melvin Richter, *The Politics of Conscience: T. H. Green and his Age*, (London: Weidenfeld and Nicolson, 1964) pp. 254–61; Henry Sidgwick, *Lectures on the Ethics of T. H. Green, Mr. Herbert Spencer and J Martineau* (London: Macmillan, 1902) pp. 69–72.

25 Avital Simhony, 'Colin Tyler, *Thomas Hill Green (1836–1882) and the Philosophical Foundations of Politics. An Internal Critique'*, *Bradley Studies*, 5:1 (1999) 87–106, p. 100.

26 Hurka, *Perfectionism*, p. 64.

27 Immanuel Kant, *The Doctrine of Virtue: Part 2 of the Metaphysics of Morals*, translated by Mary Gregor (Philadelphia: University of Pennsylvania Press, 1964) pp. 44–5. The passage is quoted by Hurka in *Perfectionism*, p. 65.

28 See Hurka's *Perfectionism*, p. 152.

29 *Prolegomena*, 251, 235.

30 *Prolegomena*, 257, 240.

31 H. A. Prichard, *Moral Obligation. Essays and Lectures* (Oxford: Clarendon Press, 1957).

32 *Ibid.*, p. 71.

33 Peter Nicholson, *The Political Philosophy of the British Idealists*, (Cambridge: Cambridge University Press, 1990) p. 66.

34 *Ibid.*, see Study II, Section II.

35 *Ibid.*, p. 66.

36 *Prolegomena*, 256, 239; 252, 235.

37 *Prolegomena*, 256, 239.

38 *Prolegomena*, 259, 241, emphasis added.

39 *Prolegomena*, 258, 240.

40 *Prolegomena*, 253, 236.

41 *Prolegomena*, 211, 200.

42 See *Prolegomena*, 104, 100.

43 *Prolegomena* 258, 240.

44 *Prolegomena*, 309, 286.

45 *Prolegomena*, 309, 286.

46 *Prolegomena*, 292, 271.

47 *Prolegomena*, 311, 288. The italics in the last sentence are mine.

48 *Prolegomena*, 311, 288.
49 Avital Simhony, 'T. H. Green: The Common Good Society', *History of Political Thought*, 14:2 (1993) 225–47.
50 See *Prolegomena*, Book III, Chapter V: 'The Greek and the Modern Conceptions of Virtue'.
51 See the Introduction, sections 3 and 4.
52 *Principles* 26, 26.

Chapter 4

1 I would like to acknowledge the help of Peter Nicholson, James Connelly, Duncan Ivison, Richard Cookson and Maria Ferretti. I have also benefited by the comments of two anonymous referees for *Political Studies*.
2 If we agree that Berlin's essay 'Two Concepts of Liberty' has started this debate, then it has lasted for more than four decades. This essay is based on an Inaugural Lecture delivered in 1958.
3 According to Pettit, republican freedom is freedom as 'non-domination'. He argues that this concept represents a third possibility which has been foreclosed by Berlin's taxonomy of positive and negative liberty. Philip Pettit, *Republicanism: A Theory of Freedom and Government* (Oxford: Clarendon Press, 1997) pp. 17–27. See also Quentin Skinner's 'The Paradoxes of Political Liberty' in *Liberty*, ed. David Miller (Oxford: Oxford University Press, 1993) pp. 183–205.
4 Peter Nicholson *The Political Philosophy of the British Idealists* (Cambridge: Cambridge University Press, 1990) p. 131.
5 Isaiah Berlin, 'Two Concepts of Liberty', in *The Proper Study of Mankind*, ed. by Henry Hardy and Roger Hausheer (London: Chatto & Windus, 1997) pp. 191–242.
6 Tom Baldwin, 'MacCallum and the Two Concepts of Freedom', *Ratio*, 26 (1984) 125–42.
7 See Raymond Plant, *Modern Political Thought* (Oxford: Basil Blackwell, 1993) p. 248; Charles Taylor, 'What's Wrong with Negative Liberty', in *The Idea of Freedom*, ed. by Alan Ryan (Oxford: Oxford University Press, 1979) pp. 175–93, p. 181.
8 Gerald MacCallum, 'Negative and Positive Freedom', in *Liberty*, ed. David Miller (Oxford: Oxford University Press, 1993) pp. 100–22.
9 See note 3.
10 T. H. Green, 'On the Different Senses of "Freedom" as Applied to Will and to the Moral Progress of Man', in *Lectures on the Principles of Political Obligation and Other Writings*, ed. by Paul Harris and John Morrow (Cambridge: Cambridge University Press, 1986) pp. 228–49. Hereafter *Freedom*; in quoting, the first figure will refer to the page number, the second, to the section number.
11 T. H. Green, 'Lecture on "Liberal Legislation and Freedom of Contract"', in *Lectures on the Principles of Political Obligation and Other Writings*, pp. 194–212. Hereafter, *Liberal Legislation*.

12 *Freedom*, 241, 17–18.
13 *Freedom*, 242, 19.
14 *Freedom*, 240, 17.
15 *Freedom*, 228, 1.
16 See sections 2.2 and 2.3.
17 See section 3.3.
18 *Freedom*, 228, 1.
19 Hillel Steiner (Steiner, 'Individual Liberty', in *Liberty*, ed. by David Miller [Oxford: Oxford University Press, 1993] pp. 123–40) argues that someone's will should have no direct bearing on deciding whether she is free or not. 'Being placed in a locked prison cell renders me unfree to go to the theatre regardless of whether I want to go to the theatre or not' (p. 125). Green's reply would be that the reason why we consider that the person in prison is not free to go to the theatre is *the possibility* that this person may want to go to the theatre. If it is not the actual will that has been limited, it is the *potential will* which renders it meaningful to speak about lack of freedom. For further discussion of the link between freedom and desire see Plant, *Modern Political Thought*, pp. 236–44, and Fred Rosen, *Thinking about Liberty: An Inaugural Lecture Delivered at the UCL* (London: University College London, 1990) p. 13.
20 *Freedom*, 242, 19.
21 *Freedom*, 241, 17.
22 *Freedom*, 241, 18.
23 MacCallum, 'Negative and Positive Freedom', p. 100.
24 '*x* is (is not) free from *y* to do (not do, become, not become) *z*, where *x* ranges over agents, *y* ranges over such 'preventing conditions' as constraints, restrictions, interferences, and barriers, and *z* ranges over actions or conditions of character or circumstance'. *Ibid.*, p. 102.
25 Baldwin, 'MacCallum and the Two Concepts of Freedom', p. 130.
26 Nicholson, *The Political Philosophy of the British Idealists*, p. 124.
27 *Freedom*, 243, 19.
28 *Freedom*, 243, 20. For further discussion of Green and the 'dualistic fallacy', see Avital Simhony, 'On Forcing Individuals to be Free: T. H. Green's Liberal Theory of Positive Freedom', *Political Studies*, 39 (1991) 303–20, pp. 309–12.
29 Nicholson, *The Political Philosophy of the British Idealists*, p. 124.
30 *Freedom*, 248, 25.
31 *Liberal Legislation*, p. 200.
32 Nicholson, *The Political Philosophy of the British Idealists*, p. 121.
33 Berlin, 'Two Concepts of Liberty', p. 204.
34 See subsection 4.1.2.
35 It has been already convincingly demonstrated by Nicholson and Simhony that Berlin's criticism of Green's positive freedom is not justifiable. See Nicholson, *The Political Philosophy of the British Idealists*, pp. 124–6; and Simhony, 'On Forcing Individuals to be Free: T. H. Green's Liberal Theory of Positive Freedom', pp. 303–6. However, it has not been pointed out that Green's defence of positive freedom diverges from his

defence of moral freedom and the moral rigour implicit in the second one is not implicit in the first.

36 *Liberal Legislation*, p. 196.
37 *Ibid.*
38 *Ibid.*, p. 197.
39 See the note of the editors Paul Harris and John Morrow, *Lectures on Principles of Political Obligation and Other Writings*, note 2, p. 343, citing *Hansard*, series 3, vol. CCLV, pp. 1975–89.
40 *Liberal Legislation*, p. 194. The Act in question was the Employers' Liability Act.
41 *Liberal Legislation*, p. 209.
42 *Ibid.*, p. 199.
43 *Ibid.*
44 *Ibid.*
45 *Ibid.*, p. 203.
46 See MacCallum, 'Negative and Positive Freedom'. Baldwin points out that long before MacCallum, Bernard Bosanquet has argued that the distinction 'from/to' does not explain the different meanings of freedom. See Baldwin, 'MacCallum and the Two Concepts of Freedom', p. 126.
47 Berlin, 'Two Concepts of Liberty', p. 199.
48 *Ibid.*, p. 197.
49 *Ibid.*
50 *Ibid.*, p. 199.
51 *Ibid.*
52 *Ibid.*, p. 196
53 *Ibid.*, p. 199.
54 *Ibid.*, p. 198.
55 See Baldwin, 'MacCallum and the Two Concepts of Freedom'; Nicholson, *The Political Philosophy of the British Idealists*, p. 121; Taylor, 'What's Wrong with Negative Liberty', pp. 175–93. Taylor's argument that negative freedom is an opportunity concept, in essence, presents negative freedom as the juristic one.
56 Baldwin, 'MacCallum and the Two Concepts of Freedom', pp. 138–42.
57 *Liberal Legislation*, p. 200.

Chapter 5

1 I am indebted to Peter Nicholson who has read successive drafts of this chapter and offered valuable comments. I am also obliged to Susan Mendus and the Political Theory Workshop of the Department of Politics, University of York.
2 T. H. Green, *Lectures on the Principles of Political Obligation* in *Lectures on the Principles of Political Obligation and Other Writings*, ed. by Paul Harris and John Morrow (Cambridge: Cambridge University Press, 1986). Hereafter, *Principles*; in quoting, the first figure will refer to the number of the page, the second, to the number of the section.

3 See sections 32–78 in the *Principles*.

4 *Principles* 91, 116.

5 *Principles*, 110, 141.

6 John Austin (1790–1859), Professor of Jurisprudence in the University of London (1826–32) and an associate of Bentham and Mill.

7 I am indebted to Peter Nicholson for making this point clear. He argues that we cannot speak about 'contradiction', but only of 'some differences of presentation' in the *Prolegomena* and in the *Principles*. He points out that rather than contradictory, the fact that Green's philosophy contains 'both historical and universalistic elements' is advantageous. In reply to his comments I can express my position in clearer terms. I believe that the two perspectives developed by Green are of great advantage to Green's philosophy but I criticise him for the fact that he does not spell out the *possibility* of contradiction between them. The possibility of such contradiction has significant impact on defining the justification of human rights.

8 Colin Tyler, *Thomas Hill Green (1836–1882) and the Philosophical Foundations of Politics* (Lewiston: The Edwin Mellen Press, 1997) pp. 169–92.

9 Peter Nicholson, *The Political Philosophy of the British Idealists* (Cambridge: Cambridge University Press, 1990) pp. 83–95.

10 Rex Martin, 'Green on Natural Rights in Hobbes, Spinoza and Locke', in *The Philosophy of T. H. Green*, ed. by Andrew Vincent (Aldershot: Gower, 1986) 104–26.

11 Geoffrey Thomas, *The Moral Philosophy of T. H. Green* (Oxford: Clarendon Press, 1987) pp. 351–6.

12 *Ibid.*, p. 352.

13 Martin, 'Green on Natural Rights in Hobbes, Spinoza and Locke', p. 104.

14 Tyler, *Thomas Hill Green (1836–1882) and the Philosophical Foundations of Politics*, p. 179.

15 Nicholson speaks of '*implicit* social recognition' and of claims 'fully and *explicitly* recognised as legal rights' (*The Political Philosophy of the British Idealists*, p. 89, emphasis added). The distinction between 'metaphysical' and 'practical' which I will argue for may be seen as corresponding to a distinction between 'implicit' and 'explicit', which has already been made; there are, however, some differences. Both the implicit and explicit recognition can be seen as aspects of what I will define as practical recognition.

16 *Principles*, 112, 143.

17 *Principles*, 113, 143.

18 *Principles*, 112, 143.

19 *Principles*, 109, 140.

20 *Principles*, 108, 139.

21 *Principles*, 110, 141.

22 *Principles*, 112, 143.

23 Nicholson, *The Political Philosophy of the British Idealists*, p. 90.

24 *Prolegomena*, 351, 321.

25 *Principles*, 26–7, 26.

26 *Principles*, 28, 29.
27 *Principles*, 36, 38.
28 *Principles*, 26–7, 26, emphasis added.
29 *Principles*, 48, 55.
30 *Principles*, 108, 139, emphasis added.
31 *Principles*, 113, 143.
32 This is the title of Part A of Chapter II of Book III of the *Prolegomena*.
33 See section 2.7 of this book.
34 *Prolegomena*, 195, 185.
35 *Prolegomena*, 193, 184.
36 *Principles*, 109, 140.
37 T. H. Green, 'The Force of Circumstances', *Works of Thomas Hill Green, Volume III*, ed. by R. L. Nettleship (London: Longmans, Green, and Co, 1889), 3–10, p. 10.
38 *Ibid.*, p. 10.
39 *Prolegomena*, 263, 245.
40 *Prolegomena*, 202, 191.
41 *Prolegomena*, 212, 201.
42 See Chapters IV and V of Book III of *Prolegomena*, entitled 'The Development of the Moral Ideal'.
43 *Principles*, 26, 26.
44 *Principles*, 26, 25.
45 See *Principles*, section 143.
46 *Prolegomena*, 190, 181.

Bibliography

1. Selected Writings by Green and Husserl

Green, T. H., *Prolegomena to Ethics* (Oxford: Clarendon Press, 1890).

___ *Lectures on the Principles of Political Obligation and Other Writings*, ed. by Paul Harris and John Morrow (Cambridge: Cambridge University Press, 1986).

___ *Works of Thomas Hill Green, Volume I*, ed. by R. L. Nettleship (London: Longmans, Green and Co., 1894).

___ *Works of Thomas Hill Green, Volume III*, ed. by R. L. Nettleship (London: Longmans, Green, and Co., 1889).

___ *Collected Works of T. H. Green, Volume 5*, ed. by Peter Nicholson (Bristol: Thoemmes Press, 1997).

___ 'Essay on Christian Dogma', *Works of Thomas Hill Green, Volume III*, pp. 161–85.

___ 'Faith', *Works of Thomas Hill Green, Volume III*, pp. 253–76.

___ 'The Force of Circumstances', *Works of Thomas Hill Green, Volume III*, pp. 3–10.

___ 'Introductions to Hume's "Treatise of Human Nature"', *Works of Thomas Hill Green, Volume I*, pp. 1–370.

___ 'Lecture on "Liberal Legislation and Freedom of Contract"', in *Lectures on the Principles of Political Obligation and Other Writings*, pp. 194–212.

___ 'On the Different Senses of "Freedom" as Applied to Will and to the Moral Progress of Man', in *Lectures on the Principles of Political Obligation and Other Writings*, pp. 228–49.

___ 'Popular Philosophy in its Relation to Life', *Works of Thomas Hill Green, Volume III*, pp. 92–125.

___ 'The Province of Ethics', in *Collected Works of T. H. Green, Volume 5*, pp. 193–4.

___ 'Review of J. Watson: "Kant and his English Critics"', *Works of Thomas Hill Green, Volume III*, pp. 147–58.

___ 'Review of E. Caird, "Philosophy of Kant"', *Works of Thomas Hill Green, Volume III*, pp. 126–37.

___ 'The Witness of God', *Works of Thomas Hill Green, Volume III*, pp. 230–52.

Husserl, Edmund, 'Fichte's Ideal of Humanity [Three Lectures]', trans. by James G. Hart, *Husserl Studies* 12 (1995) 111–33.

___ *Ideas Pertaining to a Pure Phenomenology and to a Phenomenological Philosophy, First Book*, trans. by F. Kersten (Dordrecht: Kluwer Academic Publishers, 1982).

___ *Logical Investigations*, trans. by J. N. Findlay (London: Routledge & Kegan Paul, 1970).

___ *The Crisis of European Sciences and Transcendental Phenomenology*, trans. by David Carr (Evanston, Ill: Northwestern University Press, 1970).

___ *Cartesian Meditations*, trans. by Dorion Cairns (The Hague: Martinus Nijhoff, 1960).

2.   Other sources

Allison, Henry E., 'Transcendental Analytic', *The Oxford Companion to Philosophy*, ed. by Ted Honderich (Oxford: Oxford University Press, 1995) p. 878.

Baldwin, Tom, 'MacCallum and the Two Concepts of Freedom', *Ratio* 26 (1984) 125–42.

Berlin, Isaiah, 'Two Concepts of Liberty', in *The Proper Study of Mankind*, ed. by Henry Hardy and Roger Hausheer (London: Chatto & Windus, 1997) pp. 191–242.

Bosanquet, Bernard, *The Principle of Individuality and Value* (London: Macmillan – now Palgrave, 1927).

Boys Smith, J. S., 'The Interpretation of Christianity in Idealistic Philosophy in Great Britain in the Nineteenth Century', *The Modern Churchman* 21 (1944) 251–73.

Brink, David, 'Self-Love and Altruism', *Social Philosophy & Policy* 14:1 (1997) 122–57.

Camus, Albert, *The Myth of Sisyphus*, trans. by Justin O'Brian (London: Penguin Books, 1975).

Cassirer, Ernst, *An Essay on Man* (New Haven, Conn.: Yale University Press, 1972).

___ *The Philosophy of Symbolic Forms*, trans. By Ralph Manheim, 3 vols (New Haven, Conn.: Yale University Press, 1953–7).

___ *Symbol, Myth, Culture. Essays and Lectures of Ernst Cassirer 1935–1945*, ed. by Donald Verene (New Haven, Conn.: Yale University Press, 1979).

Chubb, Percival, 'The Significance of Thomas Hill Green's Philosophical and Religious Teaching', *The Journal of Speculative Philosophy* 22:1 and 2 (1888) 1–21.

de Boer, Theodore, *The Development of Husserl's Thought* (The Hague: Martinus Nijhoff, 1978).

Descartes, René, *Meditations on the First Philosophy*, in *Key Philosophical Writings*, trans. by Elizabeth S. Haldane and G. R. T. Ross (Ware, Hertfordshire: Wordsworth Editions Limited, 1997).

Dimova, Maria, 'T. H. Green as a Phenomenologist; Linking British Idealism and Continental Phenomenology', *Angelaki: Journal of the Theoretical Humanities* 3:1 (1998) 77–88.

___ 'T. H. Green's Philosophy of Religion: A Phenomenological Perspective', *Bradley Studies* 3:2 (1997) 129–50.

Dimova-Cookson, Maria, 'T. H. Green's Theory of the Common Good', *Collingwood Studies* VI (1999) 85–109.

Francis, M. and Morrow, J., *A History of English Political Thought in the Nineteenth Century* (London: Duckworth, 1994).

Freud, Sigmund, *The Psychopathology of Everyday Life*, ed. by James Strachey, trans. by Alan Tyson (Harmondsworth: Penguin Books, 1991).

Hammond, M., Howarth, J. and Keat, R., *Understanding Phenomenology* (Oxford: Basil Blackwell, 1991).

Harris, Errol E., 'The Problem of Self-constitution for Idealism and Phenomenology', *Idealistic Studies* 7 (1977) 1–27.

Harkins, Georgia E., 'T. H. Green as a Philosopher of Religion', *The Personalist* 5 (1924) 172–8.

Hegel, G. W. F., *Elements of the Philosophy of Right*, ed. by Allen W. Wood, trans. by H. B. Nisbet (Cambridge: Cambridge University Press, 1991).

___ *Phenomenology of Spirit*, trans. by A. V. Miller (Oxford: Oxford University Press, 1977).

Hobhouse, L. T., *Liberalism* (London: Williams and Norgate, 1911).

Hume, David, *A Treatise of Human Nature*, ed. by L. A. Selby-Bigge (Oxford: Clarendon Press, 1888).

Hurka, Thomas, *Perfectionism* (Oxford: Oxford University Press, 1993).

Hylton, Peter, 'The Metaphysics of T. H. Green', *History of Philosophy Quarterly* 2:1 (1985) 91–110.

Hyppolite, Jean, *Genesis and Structure of Hegel's Phenomenology of Spirit*, trans. by Samuel Cherniak and John Heckman (Evanston, Ill.: Northwestern University Press, 1974).

Jaspers, Karl, *Philosophy of Existence*, trans. by Richard F. Graban (Philadelphia: University of Pennsylvania Press, 1971).

Lewis, H. D., 'Was Green a Hedonist?', *Mind* 45 (1936) 193–8.

Locke, John, *Two Treatises of Government*, ed. by Peter Laslett (Cambridge: Cambridge University Press, 1988).

___ *An Essay Concerning Human Understanding*, ed. by John W. Yolton (London: J. M. Dent & Sons Ltd, 1961).

Kant, Immanuel, *Critique of Pure Reason*, ed. by Vasilis Politis (London: Everyman, 1993).

___ *Critique of Practical Reason*, trans. by Lewis White Beck (Englewood Cliffs, NJ: Prentice-Hall, 1993).

___ *The Metaphysics of Morals*, trans. by Mary Gregor (Cambridge: Cambridge University Press, 1996).

MacCallum, Gerald, 'Negative and Positive Freedom', in *Liberty*, ed. David Miller (Oxford: Oxford University Press, 1993), pp. 100–22.

MacKinnon, D. M., 'Some Aspects of the Treatment of Christianity by the British Idealists', *Religious Studies* 20 (1984) 133–44.

MacPherson, C. B., *The Life and Times of Liberal Democracy* (Oxford: Oxford University Press, 1977).

Mandel, Ernest and Novack, George, *The Marxist Theory of Alienation* (New York: Pathfinder, 1995).

Martin, Rex, 'Green on Natural Rights in Hobbes, Spinoza and Locke', in *The Philosophy of T. H. Green*, ed. by Andrew Vincent (Aldershot: Gower, 1986) pp. 104–26.

Marx, Karl, *Economic and Philosophic Manuscripts of 1844*, trans. by Martin Milligan (New York: International Publishers, 1964).

___ *The Communist Manifesto*, trans. by Frederic L. Bender (New York: W. W. Norton, 1988).

McCloskey, H. J., 'The Problem of Liberalism', *The Review of Metaphysics* 19:2 (1965) 248–75.

Mill, John Stuart, *Utilitarianism*, in *On Liberty and Other Essays*, ed. by John Gray (Oxford: Oxford University Press, 1991).

___ *On Liberty* (London: Penguin Books, 1974).

Milne, Alan, 'The Common Good and Rights in T. H. Green's Ethical and Political Theory', in *The Philosophy of T. H. Green*, ed. by Andrew Vincent (Aldershot: Gower, 1986) pp. 62–75.

___ *The Social Philosophy of English Idealism* (London: Allnn & Unwin, 1962).

Morrow, John, 'Liberalism and British Idealist Political Philosophy: A Reassessment', *History of Political Thought* 5:1 (1984) 91–108.

___ 'British Idealism, "German Philosophy" and the First World War', *Australian Journal of Politics and History* 26 (1982) 380–90.

Nicholson, Peter, 'T. H. Green's Doubts about Hegel's Political Philosophy', *Bulletin of Hegel Society of Great Britain* 31 (1995) 61–72.

___ *The Political Philosophy of the British Idealists* (Cambridge: Cambridge University Press, 1990).

___ 'Religion, Philosophy and Politics in the Thought of T. H. Green', paper for the Dunn/Skinner Seminar, University of Cambridge, 1992.

___ 'Philosophical Idealism and International Politics: A Reply to Dr Savigear', *British Journal of International Studies* 2 (1976) 76–83.

Paget, Stephen, *Henry Scott Holland. Memoir and Letters* (London: John Murray, 1921).

Peterson, William, 'Gladstone's Review of *Robert Elsmere*: Some Unpublished Correspondence', *Review of English Studies* (1970) 442–61.

Pettit, Philip, *Republicanism: A Theory of Freedom and Government* (Oxford: Clarendon Press, 1997).

Plant, Raymond, *Modern Political Thought* (Oxford: Basil Blackwell, 1993).

Pople, Joy, 'Jacob and Esau; Genesis 25:19–26:5', Internet, 1998.

Prichard, H. A., *Moral Obligation. Essays and Lectures* (Oxford: Clarendon Press, 1957).

Quinton, Anthony, 'T. H. Green's "Metaphysics of Knowledge"', paper given at the conference 'Anglo-American Idealism 1865–1927', Oxford, July 1997.

___ 'Transcendentalism', in *The Oxford Companion to Philosophy* ed. by Ted Honderich (Oxford: Oxford University Press, 1995) pp. 878–9.

Richter, Melvin, *The Politics of Conscience; T. H. Green and His Age* (London: Weidenfeld and Nicolson, 1964).

___ 'T. H. Green and his Audience: Liberalism as a Surrogate Faith', *Review of Politics* 18 (1956) 444–72.

Ritchie, David G., *The Principles of State Interference* (London: Swan Sonnenschein & Co., 1896).

Rosen, Fred, *Thinking about Liberty: An Inaugural Lecture Delivered at the UCL* (London: University College London, 1990).

Rousseau, Jean-Jaques, *Discourse on the Origin of Inequality*, in *The Basic Political Writings*, trans. by Donald A. Cress (Indianapolis: Hackett Publishing Company, 1987).

___ *The Social Contract*, trans. by Maurice Cranston (London: Penguin Books, 1968).

Schutz, Alfred, *The Phenomenology of the Social World*, trans. by George Walsh and Frederik Lehnert (Evanston, Ill.: Northwestern University Press, 1967).

Seth, A., *Hegelianism and Personality* (Edinburgh & London: William Blackwood, 1887).

Sidgwick, Henry, *Lectures on the Ethics of T. H. Green, Mr. Herbert Spencer, and J. Martineau* (London: Macmillan, 1902).

Simmel, Georg, *On Individuality and Social Forms. Selected Writings*, ed. by Donald N. Levine (Chicago: The University of Chicago Press, 1971).

Simhony, Avital, Review article, 'Colin Tyler, *Thomas Hill Green (1836–1882) and the Philosophical Foundations of Politics'*, *Bradley Studies* 5:1 (1999) 87–106.

___ 'Was T. H. Green a Utilitarian?', *Utilitas* 7:1 (1995) 121–44.

___ 'T. H. Green: The Common Good Society', *History of Political Thought* 14:2 (1993) 225–47.

___ 'Beyond Negative and Positive Freedom: T. H. Green's View of Freedom', *Political Theory* 21 (1993) 28–54.

___ 'On Forcing Individuals to be Free: T. H. Green's Liberal Theory of Positive Freedom', *Political Studies* 39 (1991) 303–20.

___ 'Idealist Organicism: Beyond Holism and Individualism', *History of Political Thought* 12:3 (1991) 515–35.

___ 'T. H. Green's Theory of the Morally Justified Society', *History of Political Thought*, 10:3 (1989) 481–98.

Skinner, Quentin, 'The Paradoxes of Political Liberty', in *Liberty*, ed. by David Miller (Oxford: Oxford University Press, 1993).

Skorupski, John, *English-Language Philosophy 1750–1945* (Oxford: Oxford University Press, 1993).

Smith, Craig A., 'The Individual and Society in T. H. Green's Theory of Virtue', *History of Political Thought* 2:1 (1981) 187–201.

Smith, N. Kemp, *The Philosophy of David Hume* (London: Macmillan – now Palgrave, 1960).

Spiegelberg, Herbert, *The Phenomenological Movement* (The Hague: Martinus Nijhoff, 1982).

___ 'Husserl in Britain: Facts and Lessons', *The Journal of the British Society for Phenomenology* 1:1 (1970) 4–15.

Sprigge, T. L. S., 'Utilitarianism and Idealism: A Rapprochement', *Philosophy* 60 (1985) 447–63.

Steiner, Hillel, 'Individual Liberty', in *Liberty*, ed. by David Miller (Oxford: Oxford University Press, 1993).

Taylor, Charles, 'What's Wrong with Negative Liberty', *The Idea of Freedom*, ed. by Alan Ryan (Oxford: Oxford University Press, 1979) pp. 175–93.

Thomas, Geoffrey, *The Moral Philosophy of T. H. Green* (Oxford: Clarendon Press, 1987).

Toennies, Ferdinand, *Community and Society*, trans. by Charles P. Loomis (New York: Harper & Row, 1963).

Toynbee, Arnold, Preface to T. H. Green's *The Witness of God and Faith*, ed. by Arnold Toynbee (London: Longmans, Green, and Co, 1883), pp. iii–vii.

Tyler, Colin, *Thomas Hill Green (1836–1882) and the Philosophical Foundations of Politics* (Lewiston: The Edwin Mellen Press, 1997).

___ 'Review of Melvin Richter's *Politics of Conscience: T. H. Green and His Age*, Thoemmes Press, Bristol,' *Bradley Studies* 3:2 (1997) 192–8.

Vincent, Andrew W., 'The State and Social Purpose in Idealist Political Philosophy', *History of European Ideas* 8:3 (1987) 333–47.

___ 'T. H. Green and the Religion of Citizenship', in *The Philosophy of T. H. Green*, ed. by Andrew Vincent (Aldershot: Gower, 1986) pp. 48–61.

___ and Plant, Raymond, *Philosophy, Politics and Citizenship: The Life and Thought of the British Idealists* (Oxford: Basil Blackwell, 1984).

Walsh, W. H., 'Green's Criticism of Hume', *The Philosophy of T. H. Green*, ed. by Andrew Vincent (Aldershot: Gower, 1986) pp. 21–35.

Weinstein, David, 'Between Kantianism and Consequentialism in T. H. Green's Moral Philosophy', *Political Studies* 41:4 (1993) 618–35.

Weinstein, W. L., 'The Concept of Liberty in Nineteenth Century English Political Thought', *Political Studies* 13 (1965) 145–62.

Index

agency, human, 40–53, 140–1
  see also practice, human
agency, moral, 20–1, 56, 61–7, 69,
    76–9, 85–92
  see also good, moral; moral
      behaviour; moral ideal; needs,
      moral; vulnerability, moral
altruism, *see* noble social interest
apodictic knowledge, 15–17
  see also truth
attitude, 19–21, 34, 48, 62–4, 70, 78,
    84–6
  see also disposition; motivation

Baldwin, Tom, 106, 111, 124, 163n.
    46
Berkeley, 31
Bosanquet, Bernard, 52, 163n. 46
Brink, David, 3, 151n. 3, 159n. 23,
    159n. 60

Cassirer, Ernst, 26
cogito ergo sum, 17
common consciousness, 134–6
common good, 81–104
  formal definition of, 82, 85–92
  and freedom, 116–19
  and human rights, 137–40
  substantive definition of, 85, 100–2
  see also good, moral
consequentialism, 72–4

deontology, 72–4
Descartes, René, 17, 153n. 50
desire, 23, 25, 40–9, 56–64
determinism, spiritual, 51–3
development
  as progress, 65–7
  as self-development, 66–7, 74–8,
      85–92

as self-transformation, 2, 20–1,
    79, 103–4, 150: *see also* self-
      overcoming; self-
      transcendence
disposition, 20, 34, 64, 67–73, 78, 94
self-disinterested, 4, 16, 20–1, 57,
    62–4, 68, 70, 86, 89, 91, 149–50
  see also attitude; motivation

epistemology, 21, 24, 27–9, 32, 35,
    39, 46, 51
  see also metaphysics of knowledge
epochē, 9–21, 79, 103–4
eternal consciousness, 29, 65–6
experience, 10, 14–20, 23, 25–33,
    39, 43–4, 153n. 50, 154n. 5
  and knowledge, 27–32
  and transcendental categories,
      24–7, 45–8
  see also pre-scientific life

family, 88, 95
freedom, 105–27, 149–50
  evaluation of, 124–7
  juristic, 108–15, 123–7
  moral (or true), 108–15, 116
  and the nature of human agency,
      109–12
  negative, 120–4, 126, 143–5
  positive, 116–23
  and the will, 109–12
fulfilment, 62, 67–8, 77, 85, 89, 97,
    100, 102, 108–9, 113–14, 117,
    119–20, 123, 125, 127, 137–8,
    140–3, 146, 149

Galilean science, 11–14, 18
good, 58–63
  moral, 61–72, 107–8, 112–15, 127
    see also common good

good (*continued*)
  ordinary, 97–102, 107–8, 112–15, 127

Hegel, G. W. F., xi, 1, 111, 112
Hume, David, 8, 24, 32–9, 153n. 50, 155n. 30, 155n. 34, 156n. 36, 156n. 40–1, 156n. 44, 156n. 61
Hurka, Thomas, 3, 151n. 3, 75–6, 92
Husserl, Edmund, xi, 1–2, 5, 9–21, 152n. 22, 152n. 30, 152n. 32, 153n. 50, 152n. 53–5, 26, 33–4, 46, 155–6n. 36, 156n. 44, 79, 103
Hylton, Peter, 31

idealism, xi-xii, 1, 3, 28–9, 31
individual
  justification of individuals' right, 140–5
  the perfection of, 56, 62, 64–72, 74–7, 79, 85–7, 92–3, 114, 116, 120, 126, 140, 142–3, 149
  the social nature of, 137–40, 146–7
  the ultimate value of, 67, 74–6, 125–7, 140–1
institutions, 67, 100–2
intellect, 50–1
  see also reason

Kant, Immanuel, xi, 2, 19, 23–9, 31–3, 46, 55, 68–9, 72–4, 92, 111–13, 117, 151n. 1, 154n. 55,

life-world, 14–15
Locke, John, 29–30, 33, 37, 46, 129–30

MacCallum, Gerald, 107, 111, 120, 163n. 46
Martin, Rex, 3, 132
metaphysics
  of human practice, 25–6, 40–5, 51
  of knowledge, 3, 19, 23, 27–32, 34, 50–1
  see also practice, human

methods
  of ethics, 5–9
  of science, 1–2, 7–15, 36–9
Mill, John Stuart, 64, 74
Milne, Alan, 3, 89
moral behaviour, 55–7, 61–7, 81–3, 85–92, 137–43
  formal conditions of, 61–4, 70, 83–92
moral ideal, 64–72, 74–6, 83–5, 95, 140–1
Morrow, John, 3, 163n. 39
motivation, 8, 20, 27, 43, 56, 61–3, 70, 79, 83, 90, 103, 126, 137, 150
  see also attitude; disposition

naturalism, ethical, 106
needs, moral, 77–8, 140–5
  see also vulnerability, moral
neutrality, moral, 64, 143–4
  see also good, ordinary; freedom, juristic
Nicholson, Peter, xi, xii, 3, 94–5, 105, 111–13, 116, 162n. 35, 132, 136. 164n. 7, 164n. 15
noble social interest, 86–7, 91, 98

objectivisim, 14–5, 153n. 53

passions, 35–40
perfection, *see* individual, the perfection of
perspectives, change of, 70–2, 74–6, 125–7, 149–50
Pettit, Philip, 107, 161n. 3
phenomenological circle, 56, 67–72, 78, 93–4
phenomenological reduction, *see* epochē
phenomenology, 15–20, 60–3, 78–9, 103–4, 149–50
  see also epochē
Plant, Raymond, 3, 162n. 19
pleasure, 57–67, 69–70
practice, human, 15, 23–7, 40–53, 57–61, 90

pre-scientific life, 13–14
Prichard, H. A., 94–5
progress, *see* development, as progress

Quinton, Anthony, 29, 154n. 16,
    155n. 24

reason, 8, 24–6, 33–40, 46–8, 50,
    156n. 40, 156n. 44
relations, given by the mind, 28–31,
    33, 36–7, 48–50
religion
    divine consciousness, *see* eternal
        consciousness
    eternal life, *see* salvation argument
    religious conversion, 16, 20: *see*
        also development, as self-
        transformation; self-
        overcoming;
        self-transcendence
Richter, Melvin, 3, 160n. 24
rights, 129–47
    historical character of, 136, 143,
        145–6
    see also justification of human
        rights
Rosen, Fred, 162n. 19
Rousseau, Jean-Jacques, 129–30

sacrifice of pleasure, 89, 119, 121
    see also disposition, self-
        disinterested; self-overcoming
salvation argument, 83, 87–92
Schutz, Alfred, 2, 152n. 22
science
    the crisis of, 10–12
    critique of, 7–15, 36–9
    of ethics, 7–9
self, the uniqueness of the, 92–7
self-distinguishing principle, 29, 31,
    40–3, 59, 65, 149
self-overcoming, 20, 62–4, 68, 71, 86,
    92, 102–4, 113, 125, 133, 138–9
    see also development, as self-
        transformation; self-
        transcendence

self-satisfaction, 40–4, 58–63, 86,
    90, 92, 103, 110–11, 140–1
    see also fulfilment
self-seeking principle, 40, 43–4, 59,
    65, 98, 111, 149
self-transcendence, 79, 125
    see also development, as self-
        transformation; self-
        overcoming
Seth, A., 155n. 21
Sidgwick, Henry, 52–3
Simhony, Avital, 3, 157n. 83, 55,
    73, 91, 101, 162n. 28, 162n. 35
Skinner, Quentin, 161n. 3
Skorupski, John, 30
Smith, N. Kemp, 33, 155n. 34
social recognition, 5, 78, 130–40,
    144–5, 149, 164n. 15
Spiegelberg, Herbert, 155–6n. 36
spirit, 1–2, 5–9, 14–15, 23–5, 27, 32,
    35–6, 39–40
    world of, 24, 32, 34–6, 38
    objective, 25, 29
Sprigge, T. L. S., 60
Steiner, Hillel, 162n. 19

Taylor, Charles, 161n. 7, 163n. 55
Thomas, Geoffrey, 3, 55, 84–5, 132
transcendental philosophy, 24–7,
    45–53
transcendental reduction, *see* epochē
transcendental subjectivity, 21
truth, 7, 10–15, 20, 26, 34, 37, 153n.
    50
Tyler, Colin, xii, 3, 29, 51–2, 155n.
    21, 72, 132

utilitarianism, 1, 57–60, 64, 73
utility, consciousness of, 135

Vincent, Andrew W., 3, 84
vulnerability, moral, 76–7, 79, 141

Weinstein, David, 3, 55, 72–3
well-being, 88–9, 93, 95, 137

Printed by Printforce, the Netherlands